Artistic Techniques

WITH ADOBE® PHOTOSHOP® AND COREL® PAINTER®

Deborah Lynn Ferro

AMHERST MEDIA, INC. ■ BUFFALO, NY

I share the joy of this book with my husband Rick, who inspires me daily. He has truly helped me to see the light, to grow as a photographer, and to love life.

I would also like to thank my mother, who has always believed in me, loved me, and prayed for me. Because of you, Mom, I believed I could accomplish anything I set my mind to. A special thanks to Lori Gragg and Angela Tankersley for all their assistance in helping me get this book ready for print. To my children, family, and clients whose images make up this book, I want to thank you for helping me make it possible. And especially to Michelle and Craig for giving me the opportunity to share my passion for artistic images—thank you so much!

Published by:
Amherst Media, Inc.
P.O. Box 586
Buffalo, N.Y. 14226
Fax: 716-874-4508
www.AmherstMedia.com

Publisher: Craig Alesse
Senior Editor/Production Manager: Michelle Perkins
Assistant Editor: Barbara A. Lynch-Johnt
Editorial Assistance: Carey Anne Maines

ISBN: 1-58428-165-0
Library of Congress Card Catalog Number: 2004113801

Printed in Korea.
10 9 8 7 6 5 4 3 2 1

TABLE OF CONTENTS

by Tim Kelly (M.Photog., Craftsmen, Fellow-ASP).

*W*hen an artist truly listens to his or her own heart, the results are destined to be unique—and quite possibly amazing. The work of Deborah Lynn Ferro has become just that.

This new collection, along with the corresponding inside look and instruction, is so much more than inspiring. Deborah's images help us remember why we are artists in the first place. The broad range of treatments and presentations are a delight to the eye, containing both a "new" traditional feel and others that are really quite radical indeed. The style however, is that of a single artist who has found her way in a medium that won't stand still. And this may be her greatest accomplishment, as the greatest foil in our brave new world of digital art is the technology itself, which can often make even the accomplished fainthearted.

Appreciating the work of today's masters as much as those who came before, I still find immeasurable satisfaction in seeing former students mature artistically to this level. It remains a marvelous truth to me that artists who have made great personal investments, mastered their tools and techniques, and then create to satisfy themselves, will undoubtedly be successful in their clients' eyes. An artist doesn't *need* public acceptance, but isn't it wonderful when there *is* an appreciative audience?

I have always admonished my student artists to be unique. The best way to do that is to study and practice until your techniques are second nature. Then, be yourself. Shoot for yourself and create to please the artist within.

Deborah is an artist of this age, a giving talent with a God-given talent who is now both producing beautiful art and inspiring others to do the same.

Enjoy this wonderful new collection.

> Deborah's images help us remember why we are artists in the first place.

1. GETTING STARTED

*W*hen using Photoshop or Painter for artistic design, it is essential to have the best tools available to you with the latest, up-to-date technology to make your workflow smooth and precise.

● SOFTWARE

When purchasing software, whether Adobe Photoshop or Corel Painter, it is important that you spend the money for your own, original version. If you have borrowed your copy of either program, you will not have technical support or be able to upgrade to new versions. With Photoshop CS, you can only load the software on two computers unless you add the network or multiple-computers options that are available for an additional fee.

With the advancement of recent versions of Photoshop, more and more artwork can be achieved on photographs. With Photoshop, you have a variety of useful tools such as artistic filters, the Smudge and Liquify tools, the History Brush, and many other tools to enhance a photograph to a more painterly representation.

However, Painter has more realistic, natural-media brushes and a wider variety of textures not offered in Photoshop. With Painter, you can paint with unlimited freedom of expression. One minute you can work with oils and the next with watercolor, allowing you to produce advanced tech-

The choice to purchase a Mac (left) or a PC (right) is a personal decision. Both Photoshop and Painter will operate from either platform.

niques that are not practical with traditional painting, such as combining media.

In order to work in Painter, you should have a working knowledge of Photoshop. With the advancements included in recent versions of Painter, it has now become easier than ever to transition between the two programs. And don't worry—Photoshop and Painter files can be exchanged between both programs.

● COMPUTER

If you are just starting out and have not yet purchased a computer, make sure that you get the most hard drive space, processor speed, and RAM that you can afford. The choice to purchase a PC or Mac is a personal decision; however, both Photoshop and Painter will operate from either platform. If you use a Windows system, it should have Windows 2000 or Windows XP, at the *very* least 256MB of RAM, and a 24-bit color display with a minimum 1024 x 768 resolution.

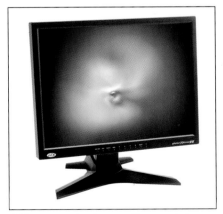

CRT monitors (top) generally provide better color and resolution than LCD monitors (above).

● MONITOR

When choosing a monitor, a CRT monitor will, in most cases, give you better color and resolution than an LCD monitor. I prefer to work with two monitors, a CRT 22-inch LaCie Monitor for the primary image display, and a secondary flat LCD monitor for my tools. This enables me to move between the two monitors when working in either program, while maximizing the size of the image I am working with on the CRT monitor. The reason that I prefer the LaCie CRT monitor is because of its incredible color accuracy and resolution. It also has a hood screen that shields the screen from any light spill.

It is important that you calibrate your monitor on a regular basis, because monitors change their color range on a daily basis; however, the average eye will not see the change. Your monitor should also be calibrated to whatever output source you choose. The calibration that we use for all of our monitors at Signature Studio is the Fuji Color Kit Profiler.

◉ GRAPHICS PEN AND TABLET

An essential tool for any artistic design or retouching is a graphics pen and tablet. The pressure-sensitive graphics pen allows you to operate as an artist does with a pen, pencil, or brush. It enables you to draw or paint with precise detail. Imagine trying to retouch the eyeliner or eyelashes of a female portrait with a mouse—it's like working with a rock or a bar of soap! With Corel Painter,

A graphics pen and tablet are essential for artistic design and retouching.

having a graphics pen enables you to paint with brush strokes similar to traditional painting. There are several graphic pens and tablets on the market, but my preference is the Wacom Intuous Tablet and pen. The tablet I work with the most is 9 x 12 inches in size, so I can place it in my lap and paint with long strokes, as I used to on watercolor paper.

◉ COLOR SPACE

On your computer, colors can be scientifically measured and precisely matched, which is essential when looking at the reproduction of an art piece. The color in your images, however, will also be created, edited, and viewed on a series of different devices that all have their own ways of recording, handling, and displaying color. Although a complete discussion on the complicated topic of color management is beyond the scope of this book, it's important to keep a few basic concepts in mind.

First, remember that different devices in your workflow use different color models to create color. Your monitor, for example, produces color using red, green, and blue light (the RGB color model). Your printer, on the other hand, produces color using cyan, magenta, yellow, and black inks (the CMYK color model). As a result, some colors can be viewed on screen that cannot be produced by the printer, and some colors can be produced by the printer that cannot be displayed on a monitor.

Even when two devices use the same color model, they will have different color spaces—a different range of colors that can be produced or displayed. For example, both CRT and LCD monitors use RGB to produce colors, but because they use different means to display those colors, a specific red value would look different on the LCD monitor than on the CRT monitor. Even devices of the same brand and model frequently display colors differently, since it's nearly impossible for two devices to be identical due to the limitations of manufacturing and materials.

Now, let's talk about the sRGB color space—the one that professional photographers should use throughout their workflow when printing with a professional lab. All 35mm-format digital cameras capture images in the sRGB color space (*note:* Some digital 35mm-format models do allow you to set the camera to a different color space using the camera's menu options), and professional labs only print in sRGB color space. If you change your color space to anything other than sRGB, it will be necessary for the lab to change the color space *back* to sRGB in order to print, and this will negatively affect your printed image. This does not apply to large-format digital cameras (i.e. digital backs, etc.) or to images you print to your own inkjet printers—where you may be using the Adobe 1998 color space and ICC profiles specific to your printer. If you have been advised to change your color space to Adobe 1998, and you are using a 35mm digital camera to create images you'll output at a professional lab, check your manual and call your lab to verify this information.

● EDUCATION

Last but not least, don't forget about education. Staying up-to-date on all the latest technology is difficult if you don't set aside time to learn new techniques. When I first purchased Photoshop, I was self-taught—until I heard of the National Association of Photoshop Professionals (NAPP), started by Scott Kelby. Attending my first NAPP convention was very exciting and made my head swim, but the information provided made it all worthwhile. Whether you attend a hands-on class on Photoshop or Painter, go to a convention, or pick up a book (like this one), make it a practice to try out the exercises immediately while the information is new and fresh. Try to spend three hours a week experimenting with new techniques or watching an instructional DVD or tutorial. It is a never-ending learning process, but the end result will be gratifying artistically—and it will add dollars to your pocket!

> Try to spend three hours a week experimenting with new techniques.

2. THE DIGITAL FINE-ART PRINT

$\mathcal{W}$hat defines the fine-art print? Is photography considered to be fine art? And how does it compare to fine-art paintings? With the introduction of image-manipulation programs like Photoshop and Painter, we are also seeing a new entrant in the fine-art field: the digital fine-art print. If you think that we, in the digital age, are the first ones facing such questions, think again! A quick look at art history reveals that this evolution has been a part of the art world for a long, long time.

Before photography, a person's likeness was captured by means of an artistic painted portrait. Commissioning an artist to do a portrait was, by and large, a luxury available only to the affluent. To control costs, in fact, an expensive artist would sometimes be commissioned to paint the face and hands, while a less expensive artist would be hired to paint the subject's body.

When photography became widely used, traditional artists soon found themselves looking for new means of expression that would generate new interest among the public. With the fear that the invention of photography would take away their livelihood, artists decided to take a different approach. If *photographers* could capture an exact likeness, then *artists* would leave more to be interpreted by the viewer. As a result, less realistic and more impressionistic styles became prevalent.

Of course, a photographer is an artist—but instead of using a paintbrush he uses a camera, and instead of paint he uses light. Today, however, through the world of digital artistry, photography and traditional art

This image has been manipulated in Photoshop. The original image, taken several years ago in Stowe, Vermont, was very overexposed and unusable. Using Photoshop, several steps were taken to enhance it. This included adding a new sky, adding color in the trees, darkening the contrast and color using the Burn tool, and oversharpening the image using a technique illustrated on page 110. The final result is a beautiful image.

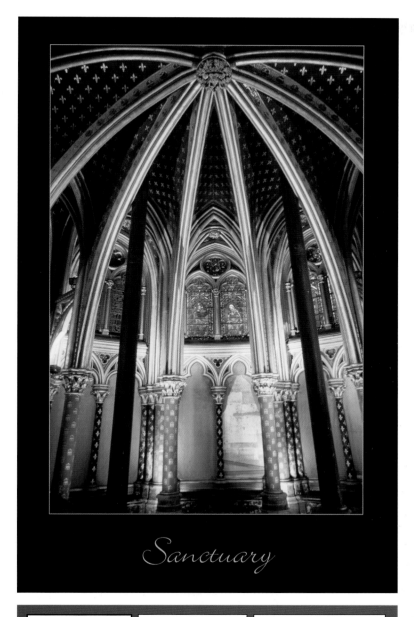

Sanctuary

ELEMENTS OF ART	PRINCIPLES OF ART	MERIT PRINT ELEMENTS
• Color	• Balance	• Impact
• Form	• Emphasis	• Creativity
• Line	• Contrast	• Style
• Shape	• Proportion	• Composition
• Space	• Pattern	• Image presentation
• Texture	• Rhythm	• Color balance
• Value	• Unity	• Center of interest
	• Variety	• Lighting
		• Subject matter
		• Image quality
		• Technique
		• Storytelling

applications have become integrated as never before to produce a new form of fine art called the digital fine-art print.

The answer, then, to what defines "fine art" is left open to interpretation. An additional factor, whether there is a demand for the digital fine-art print, depends on a variety of factors—from artistic mastery to marketing skills.

● DOES THE MEDIUM MATTER?

My philosophy is that art is an expression of your creative talent and, therefore, represents you. The medium you use to express your creativity is merely a tool and not the actual artwork. You don't disregard a writer if he uses a typewriter instead of a pen. If the smell of paint is what you seek, then by all means paint traditionally. Why not even combine the two mediums together? As humans, we have only begun to tap into a very small percentage of the creativity that our brains are capable of. Whatever opinion you hold, have fun with your artistic talent and be willing to try new ways of expressing yourself creatively.

● ELEMENTS OF A FINE-ART PRINT

There are many similarities between traditional art and photography. Compare the elements and principles of art to the elements that qualify a photo to be a merit print under the universal guidelines of print competition or when achieving a Professional Photographers of America Master's degree.

● TYPES OF FINE-ART PRINTS

In the art world there are three types of photographic prints considered to fall into the category of the "fine-art print." They are the photographic print, the digital print, and the lithographic print. The photographic prints are original straight prints and any manipulation is done by hand. The digital print is printed from a digital file, but can originate from either a digital or film capture. The lithographic print is a commercially mass-produced print.

There are a variety of ways to print your digital art piece—from traditional watercolor paper to canvas. Giclée prints, created with an Iris Printer (a specialized, high-end type of inkjet) on watercolor paper, are the predominant type of digital prints shown in galleries and have become the standard among photographers and digital artists today. "Giclée" is actually a French word and was picked by Jack Duganne in 1991 to describe the fine-art print produced from an Iris inkjet printer. He felt this was necessary because of the perception of the word "inkjet print," which, for a lot of

people, means "cheap" or "something anyone could do." Duganne wanted to raise the level of perception among the art consumer.

Of course, digital art pieces can also be produced in house. If you decide to do this, consider applying a varnish to each finished piece that won't be displayed behind glass. In addition to helping to protect the delicate surface of your image, the varnish will typically enhance the brightness, saturation, and contrast of your work. There are also a variety of wonderful papers out there that you can sample and try. So do your research and decide which paper elevates your artwork and best represents your expertise.

This image of Sacre Coeur (Paris, France) was captured on film, scanned, and then manipulated in Photoshop to create a digital fine-art print. The color saturation was enhanced by selecting areas of the image with the Magic Wand tool and increasing the saturation by choosing Image>Adjustments>Hue/Saturation. The next step was to add a Dry Brush filter by choosing Filters>Artistic>Dry Brush. The final design was printed on watercolor paper.

3. BASIC TIPS FOR PHOTOSHOP

*a*s you begin to work on your images in Photoshop and Painter, there are a few basic techniques you will find beneficial—and find yourself using time and again. These techniques, as well as some basic strategies for working in both programs, are included in this and the following chapter.

There are a few basic techniques you will find yourself using time and again.

● A GOOD ORIGINAL

When getting started, having the best possible image to work with allows you to spend more time artistically altering or retouching the images and little (if any) time color correcting the image for improper exposure. Therefore, getting the image correctly exposed before bringing it into Photoshop (and then, perhaps, on to Painter) is imperative. If you are shooting digitally, this means you will need to be extremely rigorous in your metering and exposure techniques, since digital has a lower contrast range and exposure latitude than film. There are many excellent books devoted to exposure and color correction, so if you are struggling with this aspect of photography, you should consider consulting one or more.

If the image is acquired from an outside source, make sure that you have the best possible scan or digital file to work with and that any color correction needed has been achieved before trying any of the examples in this book.

● PHOTOSHOP TIPS WHEN STARTING AN ART PRINT DESIGN

When starting an art-print project, the following are a few good Photoshop techniques to keep in mind:

1. **Always work on a PSD file; be sure to work in layers.** Working in layers and preserving these layers when you save your file makes it

easy to correct mistakes, refine your image, and continue to fine-tune your work over the course of a number of image-editing sessions.

2. **Save and save often.** Believe it or not, computers do crash—and they'll usually do it just as you wrap up a long session working on an image!

3. **Start an action to record every step.** As described on pages 17–18, you can use actions to record your work, making it easier to replicate a series of steps that create a look you like.

4. **Use Adjustment Layers and Layer Masks.** These handy tools give you an amazing degree of control over your images. Consult any

These handy tools give you an amazing degree of control . . .

This is a wonderful example how a beautiful image (above) can be made better by simply darkening it using the Curves or Levels tool on an adjustment layer (right). When using an adjustment layer, you maintain control over the image and can always revert back to the original. Here, the final image was darkened to make the background far less distracting.

basic Photoshop book for tips on using them and they'll soon become a critical part of your image-editing arsenal.

5. **When using filters, combine and alter them so that your image does not look automated.** Savvy viewers of digital images know exactly what an image looks like when any of Photoshop's filters are applied individually. Combining and altering the filters produces a more creative, customized look.

● INCREASING THE CANVAS SIZE

If you are used to shooting with a square film format and make the switch to photographing with a digital camera that is in a 35mm format, the new rectangular aspect ratio of your images can be hard to get used to. As a result, you may find that you have very little space around your subject. If you wish to crop the image square, you'll need to give the subject some room by moving back or using different lenses. If that's not possible, you can still change the size of your canvas and turn the image into a square format. The instructions for this technique are as follows.

1. In Photoshop, open the desired image with a vertical format.
2. Maximize the image to fit the screen.
3. Choose the Crop tool and, in the Options bar, activate the Clear option.

The original image (above) was nice, but adding space around the subject (left) produced a more powerful composition.

4. Crop along the borders of the entire image and extend the side of the crop indicator out beyond the left and right borders of the image until you have created a square shape.

5. Double click within the image to crop it.

6. At this point, you will see that additional space will appear in the areas where you dragged the crop indicator outside the original edges of the frame. The color of this area will be whatever the background color was set to in your Toolbar—but don't worry, we'll change that!

7. Next, choose the Rectangular Marquee tool and make a selection from the top to the bottom of the image including the background only—not the subject. Get as much of the background as you can.

8. Hit Ctrl/Cmd + T to transform your selection. A transform indicator with handles will appear. Click on a handle and drag it out from the center of the image to stretch the background to fill the new canvas area. Double click within the box to apply the transformation.

9. If necessary, repeat steps 7 and 8 on the other side of your image until you have expanded the background to cover the new canvas.

10. At this point, you may want to clean up the background with the Patch tool so that it will look as seamless as possible.

11. Go back to the Crop tool and crop the image to the precise dimensions needed.

Keep in mind that, because of the stretching and distorting, this technique can only be used on images with a studio or solid background. Obviously, this technique will not work on an environmental image.

● TRACKING YOUR WORK

How many times have you sat at the computer, experimented with an image, and come up with a wonderful result—only to find that you can't remember everything you did to get there? Sure, you can go back to your History palette and write down your steps, but a more efficient way is to

In the image above, you can see that the tricycle touched the bottom of the image and the subject was crowded in the frame. By increasing the canvas, space was created to make a more appropriate 8 x 10-inch print. The final image was then presented in sepia tone (right).

create an action when you start the image and stop recording it when you finish. Then you can print out the actions in your word processor. I suggest you keep a three-ring notebook handy with all of your favorite creative actions in it. Instructions for printing an action are as follows:

1. Go to My Documents and create a New Folder called Photoshop Actions (this is the folder in which you will save any actions that you want to print).
2. Open the image that you want to work on.
3. Go to the Actions palette.
4. Create a New Set of actions by clicking on the right drop-down arrow in the palette.
5. Name the new set.
6. In the same drop-down menu, click on New Action. (At this point you have the option to name your action and assign it a function key, which is probably not necessary unless you are planning to save this action for use in the future on another image. Actions are typically used to reduce production time on processes you perform on a regular basis.)
7. At the bottom of the Actions palette, click on the Record button. Begin working on the image.
8. When your work on the image is complete, go to the bottom of the Actions palette and click on the Stop button.
9. Hold down the Ctrl + Alt and select Save Actions from the drop-down menu in the Actions palette.
10. In the Save box, which will pop up, simply rename the action and save it into the new folder you made in step 1.
11. Go to Microsoft Word, or any word processor, and go to File>Open, identify your Saved Actions file, and open it.
12. Simply print as normal.

Corel Painter also allows you to record your steps and play them back through scripts similar to Photoshop's actions.

Keep a three-ring notebook handy with all of your favorite creative actions in it.

4. BASIC TIPS FOR PAINTER

When it comes to natural media, no digital artistry program can compare to Corel Painter—it's the only software on the market that gives you all the tools needed to create a digital work of art that is actually comparable to a traditional sketch or painting. With more than four hundred predefined brushes and the ability to use chalk, pastels, watercolors, oils, crayons, pencils, felt pens, ink, and more, your creative capability is limitless! Painting strokes can be undone with the click of a button, and endless changes can be achieved while keeping the original image intact. Painter can be compared to a well-supplied artist's studio—but with no mess or clean-up.

Before photography became a tool for my artistic expression, I had sold commission pieces of my pen-and-ink sketches and watercolor paintings. I had also trained and worked as a makeup artist for Chanel cosmetics. Both experiences influenced my approach to digital artistry. There are times when I see an image in my head before I capture it in the camera. Sometimes, though, the camera is not enough for the final creative expression. With Painter, I can translate my artistic vision into a work of art.

Endless changes can be achieved while keeping the original image intact.

● PAINTER TIPS WHEN STARTING AN ART PRINT DESIGN

When starting an art-print project, the following are a few good Painter techniques to keep in mind:

1. **Do all color correction and retouching to the image in Photoshop before bringing it into Painter.** These are the kinds of corrections Photoshop is designed for, so you'll find powerful tools there for making this type of adjustments to your photograph.

2. **Add a white canvas around the image so that you will have plenty of room to paint beyond the original edges of the image.** This

produces the most natural artistic look, without an artificially sharp edge.

3. **Always work on a cloned copy of the original photograph by going to File>Clone.** As with any digital imaging, working on a duplicate file makes it easy to start over if need be.

4. **Save the file in Painter's native file format, called RIFF.** This allows files with layers to be reopened in Painter so you can continue to work on them in future editing sessions.

5. **Save versions of your work in progress as RIFF files.** Give each version a consecutive number so you can effortlessly backtrack through the history of an image. Be sure to save a version just before flattening (eliminating the layers) for final output.

● PHOTOSHOP FILES

One of the benefits of Painter is that it works seamlessly with Photoshop— you can open Photoshop files in Painter and Painter files in Photoshop. In fact, Painter's work area is very similar to Photoshop's main work window. Talk about ease for those of us who are familiar with Photoshop! You can edit and retouch an image in Photoshop, then take it into Painter and turn it into a beautiful oil painting that can be printed on canvas. You can even create sketches from photographs. Never before has it been easier for a photographer to enhance his or her photos—and turn it into profit!

● PAINTER: A BRIEF OVERVIEW

As you'll see, there are many similarities between Photoshop and Painter. The layout of the Painter work space is similar to the one found in Photoshop, with the Toolbar on the left, the Layers and Channels palettes to the right, and options for the specific tools at the top. In Painter, as with Photoshop, you can customize your palettes and only keep open the ones you need to work on the current image, so you can maximize your workspace. Both programs also recognize most universal keyboard shortcuts.

The variety of brushes and selection of media available in Painter is incredible. You can custom build your own brushes in the Brush Creator or mix custom colors and store them for use again and again. Obviously the ease, freedom, and cross-mixing of mediums surpasses that of traditional painting. For example, true dimensional texture can be achieved through the Impasto brushes and liquid ink. Any of the brushes or blenders that include grain in their title will also add texture by controlling how much color embeds in the paper.

One of the benefits of Painter is that it works seamlessly with Photoshop.

In the Toolbar, a variety of paper textures are available, such as French Watercolor, Italian Watercolor, and Coarse Cotton Paper. These papers work well with the Chalk, Blender, and Charcoal brushes. You can even scan your own art papers and save them for creative effects.

In Painter (as in Photoshop), layers are available, making it easy to edit your work. Shape and text layers are vector-based, while default layers are raster-based (pixels). Painter's unique watercolor layers hold "wet" information, which looks like watercolor running down the canvas. As long as it is saved in this unique watercolor layer, and in RIFF format, it will be editable later. Liquid ink layers are also unique. They contain three-dimensional height information that, when saved in the RIFF format, will also remain editable.

● SAMPLE PROJECTS WITH PAINTER: GARDEN OF LIFE

The images in the sample projects that follow are straight photographic prints that were painted digitally using Painter.

The image to the left was captured with film at the Chelsea Garden Show, held in London every May. This is an annual show to display the works of landscape designers, floral artists, crafters, etc. It is a wonderful opportunity to capture beautiful stock-photography images. Even though the still life was beautiful as a straight print, I wanted to make it look like a painting. To accomplish this, the image was scanned into Photoshop using the Nikon 8000 scanner. It was then color corrected and taken into Painter, where the following techniques were used.

Original image (Garden of Life).

Figure 1.

Figure 2.

Figure 3.

1. Working on a cloned copy (File>Clone) of the original image saved as a RIFF file, I chose to add colored chalk to the image by first sampling a color from the original image with the Eyedropper tool.
2. After sampling a color from one of the vegetables, I bumped up the color's value in the Color palette.
3. Using the Square Chalk variant from the Chalk brushes (figure 1), I began to add additional color and texture to the image. (The texture was added by choosing Italian Watercolor Paper [figure 2] from the Paper Textures in the Toolbar.)
4. I continued to select various colors with the Eyedropper tool, then returned to the Square Chalk variant to add color and texture to the entire image.
5. The chalk was blended using the Grainy Blender 30 variant (found under the Blender brushes) at 100 percent opacity (figure 3).

6. Seeds were added for detail using the Texturizer-Heavy variant in the Impasto brushes.

7. Texture was added by going to Effects>Apply Surface Texture (figure 4).

8. The final image was saved as a TIFF file and brought back into Photoshop.

9. The saturation was increased by going to Image>Adjustments> Hue/Saturation.

10. Additional texture was created by going to Filter>Artistic>Rough Pastel.

11. The final filter added for texture was Filter>Noise (set to Gaussian).

12. The image was printed on Epson Watercolor Paper.

Figure 4 (above). final image (below).

It is hard to the see the quality of the texture from viewing the image as it is presented here in book form (right), but the final watercolor print is a true representation of a digital fine-art print.

● SAMPLE PROJECTS
WITH PAINTER: FULL OF LIFE

For this image, the basic steps are similar to the ones I used to paint the previous image. With each image, of course, different brushes, paper, and blenders must be used to achieve the desired effects. In this case, I took the additional step, before bringing this image into Painter, of increasing the head size of the woman (see original image on the facing page). This helped prevent her from looking distorted when brush strokes and texture were added.

After increasing the woman's head size, I placed the image on a larger white background and brought it into Painter. I used a

Original image (Full of Life).

Figure 5.

Figure 6.

Figure 7.

Final image (Full of Life).

combination of cloners and brushes to paint the image. The instructions are as follows:

1. Choose File>Clone (figure 5).
2. Choose Ctrl/Cmd + A to select the entire image.
3. Choose Delete/Backspace. This will clear your canvas.
4. Hit Ctrl/Cmd + T to activate the tracing paper. At this point, you will see the image showing through from underneath (figure 6).
5. The next step was to bring back some of the original image using the Cloner brushes (figure 7), then to add color on top of the photograph. After blending the color, I returned to the Cloner brushes to bring back in the original photograph for some additional detail.

The following is a list of the tools used.

Cloner
- Soft Cloner variant from the Cloner brushes to bring back a slight representation of the original image

Brushes
- Square Chalk variant to add color
- Detail Oils 10 variant from the Oil brushes to add detail
- Marbling Rake variant from the Distortion brushes for areas of the skirt and suitcase

Blenders
- Grainy Blender 20 variant from the Blender brushes
- Grainy Water Blender variant from the Blender brushes (size: 16.9, opacity: 23 percent, grain: 74 percent)
- Grainy Blender 30 variant from the Blender brushes to soften the edges of the portrait into the white canvas.

Papers
- Italian Watercolor Paper

Original image for Petit Mademoiselle (left). Final image (right).

● SAMPLE PROJECTS WITH PAINTER: PETIT MADEMOISELLE

In the original image of this little girl (above), the flowers are in front of her hair. The bench has been cropped so tightly that you do not see it fully. In Photoshop, I increased the canvas size of the image to add room for the bench and used the Clone tool to add areas of the flowers and bench before bringing the image into Painter. Not only is this a beautiful portrait of a little French girl, it could easily be used as a stock image for greeting cards.

Tools Used:

Brushes
- Square Chalk variant from the Chalk brushes to add color and to paint out the flowers that overlapped her hair
- Detail Oils Brush 10 variant from the Oil brushes for detail
- Smeary Bristles variant from the Distortion brushes to add texture to the wood and grass
- Texturizer-Fine variant from the Impasto brushes for the geraniums

Blenders
- Grainy 10 variant from the Blender brushes (size: 37.8, opacity: 15 percent)
- Grainy Water Blender variant from the Blender brushes (size: 16.9, opacity: 23 percent, grain: 74 percent). (*Note:* this is the only Blender I used on the face.)

- Grainy Blender 30 variant from the Blender brushes to soften the edges of the portrait into the white canvas.

Papers ■ French Watercolor Paper

● SAMPLE PROJECTS WITH PAINTER: VINE COTTAGE

Here, I added some flowers in Painter to make the image more appealing.

Tools Used:

Brushes ■ Square Chalk variant from the Chalk brushes to add color

■ Detail Oils Brush 10 variant from the Oil brushes to add detail

■ Smeary Bristles variant from the Distortion brushes to add texture

■ Texturizer-Fine variant from the Impasto brushes for the roses

Blenders ■ Grainy 10 variant from the Blender brushes (size: 37.8, opacity: 15 percent)

■ Grainy Water Blender variant from the Blender brushes (size: 16.9, opacity: 23 percent, grain: 74 percent).

Papers ■ Italian Watercolor Paper

Original image for Vine Cottage (top) and final image (above).

● ADDITIONAL PAINTER TECHNIQUES

When first starting in Painter, it is easy to become overwhelmed, so I suggest that you start with a simple image of a landscape. Then, practice adding color and blending before advancing to painting on a portrait. This is a great way to get comfortable with the brushes, variants, and paper textures available in Painter.

5. CLASSIC PORTRAITURE TURNED INTO A PAINTING

*T*he qualities that define the "classic" style of portraiture, whether painted or photographic, are based on the work of master artists such as Rembrandt and Renoir. Rembrandt was known for his rich colors, fine detail, and intimate portraits (and most photographers, when

The qualities that define the "classic" style of portraiture are based on the work of master artists.

The goal is to make the photograph look *less* realistic and *more* impressionistic.

learning classic portraiture, still learn how to create a style known as Rembrandt lighting). Renoir, on the other hand, was known for portraits that were full of life, light, and realism. Of course, *many* artists have influenced the art of photography. For that reason alone, spending time in museums or looking in art books at the library will enhance your artistic vision as a photographer. Whether you are using Photoshop, Painter, or some other creative tool to transform your photographs into works of art, it is always helpful to go back and learn from the masters.

● CREATE AN ARTISTIC IMPRESSION

Years ago, an art teacher expressed to me that, when painting, you want to create an artistic impression of what you are trying to show rather than a precise photographic representation. The more precise to reality a work of art is, the less is left to the imagination. It is interesting that, today, we are talking about much the same thing: using exact photographic imagery and translating that into art by leaving more to the imagination. So don't be afraid to be free in your artistic renderings of your photographs. If you paint a still life and make an exact copy of what a bowl of fruit looks like, you will not leave any room for artistic interpretation. It will merely be a painting of a bowl of fruit.

Also, keep in mind that the more realistic the image is, the more critical the viewer's eye will be. When an image looks very realistic, the viewer is more likely to perceive the flaws or lack of perfection. "That's not an apple," they'll say. The less realistic and more interpretive the image, however, the more the viewer has to use his imagination—and as a result, his perception will change to, "Oh, that looks like an apple!"

So the goal, when doing digital artistry is to make the photograph look *less* realistic and *more* impressionistic—evoking emotion, wonder, and self-interpretation from the viewer.

● PAINTING TECHNIQUES

When using Painter to paint on a photograph (as opposed to manipulating the image in Photoshop), I generally choose one of two methods: painting right on a cloned copy of the photograph, or cloning the image and using tracing paper for sketching, cloning, or as a guide (see pages 22–23 for an example of this technique).

For portraits, I generally paint on the cloned photograph, never working on the original. The brushes I tend to use for adding color are the Chalks and Oils. For blending, I prefer the Grainy Water variant.

When photographing a wedding, sometimes you dash to capture a spontaneous moment. In this image of a little flower girl, I tried to capture her expression so quickly that the end result was that the image was out of focus (above). As a straight photograph, I could never sell this to the client. By taking it into Painter, though, I was able to create an endearing portrait of this little girl (left).

For texture, I like the Coarse Cotton, French Watercolor, and Italian Watercolor papers. I also add additional texture to the image by going to Effects>Surface Control>Apply Surface Texture. It is important to add texture to produce a more realistic look that simulates the building up of paint. Otherwise, the final print appears soft and mushy.

While there will be significant variations from image to image, the following steps give you a quick overview of the process used to turn a photographic portrait into a painted one.

1. Choose File>Clone.
2. With the Eyedropper tool, sample a color from the original image and bump up its value in the Color palette.
3. Apply color to the image by using Chalk and Oil brushes.
4. Blend the paint using the Grainy Water Variant of the Blender brushes.
5. Blend the hard edges of the image into the white canvas using the Grainy 30 variant of the Blender brushes.

● SAMPLE PROJECTS WITH PAINTER: BRIDAL PORTRAIT

Painted bridal portraits are a wonderful additional to a high-end photography studio. When starting out, I always add a white canvas border around the image so that I am not confined to the edges of the photograph as I paint.One of my favorite techniques is to use the Grainy Blender 30 variant of the Blender brushes to soften the outer edges of the photograph and smooth them into the white canvas. If the image is first cloned by choosing File>Clone, the original image can be softly restored to blend in with the brushstrokes by using the Soft Clone variant of the Cloners brushes.

You have to be very careful when blending the paint on a portrait or you will end up smearing the pixels too much. It's best to choose a small brush, set it to a low opacity, and work in small, circular strokes. At first, it may seem difficult to achieve smooth, painterly brushwork, but with time and practice, it is easily learned.

Tools Used:

Brushes ■ Square Chalk variant of Chalk brushes (size: 9.6, opacity: 11 percent, grain: 68 percent).

Blenders ■ Soft Blender Stump 10 variant of the Blender brushes (size: 10, opacity: 21 percent, grain: 93 percent).

■ Grainy Water variant of Blender brushes (small brush size, opacity: 100 percent, grain, 80 percent)

Original image (below) and final image (bottom).

● SAMPLE PROJECTS WITH PAINTER: BROTHER AND SISTER

This image of a brother and sister (right) was cropped from a group shot at a wedding. The image was overexposed and didn't work as a straight print. Because I loved the expression and the innocence of the two children, I wanted to work on the image in Painter. With Painter, you don't even need to remove the background from the subjects, just paint it out. The techniques for painting a portrait, as discussed above, were used on this image.

● SAMPLE PROJECTS WITH PAINTER: THE AGE OF INNOCENCE

To create this portrait (facing page), I began by increasing the canvas size of the original image to give me a square format. (See page 15 for how to increase the canvas size of an image.) In this case, stretching the canvas also stretched the tree that was painted on the background of the canvas. So in Photoshop, I made a selection of the tree trunk and copied it to its own layer (Ctrl/Cmd + J). I then used the Free Transform command

Original image for Brother and Sister (top) and final image (above).

(Edit>Free Transform) on the trunk, flipping it horizontally and changing its perspective to fit in more naturally with the rest of the tree. Because this was a portrait of a child, very little retouching needed to be made to the image prior to bringing it in to Painter.

1. In Painter, open the desired image.
2. Clone the image (File>Clone), then save it as a RIFF file.
3. Maximize the window of the image.
4. You should work at a 100-percent view so that you will know exactly what your final result will be. It is very easy to overdo an image in Painter.
5. Begin by selecting the Tapered Artist Chalk 20 variant of the Chalk brushes to begin painting.
6. In the Color palette, select white as the foreground color and use the Chalk media selected in step 5 to add white highlights to the face above the eyebrows, under the eyes, around the mouth, and in the whites of the eyes.
7. Go back to the Color palette and select soft pastel colors, one at a time, to add to the white of the dress and hair bow. Light picks up

Original image for The Age of Innocence (above) and final image (right).

different colors, so to make the picture more painterly, you need to add dimension to the white. If you don't, it will look flat.

8. Next, paint in leaves on the tree background, in various shades of green, using the same Chalk brush.

9. Select the Grainy Water variant of the Blender brushes. Set it to 100-percent opacity, 80-percent grain, and a small brush size—7 percent or less. Use this brush to smooth out the areas on the dress, face, and leaves, blending the image to make it appear more painterly.

10. To add highlights and color to the hair, activate the Eyedropper tool and use it to sample a color in the hair, then go to the Color palette and adjust this color, picking a slightly lighter shade and brighter tone of the same color.

11. Paint using the Artist Pastel Chalk variant of the Chalk brushes, adding color and highlights to the hair. Repeat step 10 to smooth in the highlights.

In this image, the same techniques were used as described above. Color was added to the background using Chalk brushes and the emblem on her shirt was removed by painting over it. Finally, highlights were added to her hair.

The appearance of text on your images, promotional material, and advertisements can have a direct impact on your clients' perception of you, your studio, and the effectiveness of the photography that you are trying to market. It may be hard to believe, but you can directly affect your clients' buying decisions with the size, font style, and color of your text.

The fonts you select should be legible and comfortable to read.

Baby Parts

Signature Studio

by Rick & Deborah Ferro

904.288.6464   **www.rickferro.com**

● FONT SIZE

First, let's talk about the size of your font. You don't want it to be too big or too small. Use larger text for the words or phrases that you want to emphasize. The one thing that you *don't* want is to overwhelm the client with *all* large font. Yes, you want to grab their attention and you want impact . . . but don't shout at them with huge, over-the-top fonts that will confuse them and turn them away from your product. On the other hand, you don't want text that is too small. Eye strain is not a good marketing tool! Your goal should be to use text that is legible and comfortable for the client to read. One other issue regarding font size: don't use ALL CAPS. Text set all in capitals is hard to read and, if used in the wrong way, looks unprofessional. The one way you *may* want to use caps is in the headline of your marketing piece. More often than not, however, using all capitals is perceived as yelling or screaming at your clients, begging for their attention.

● FONT STYLE

Another issue with text is the style that you choose for your font. One mistake a lot of individuals make is using the wrong style font for what they are trying to sell—for instance, using a comical font to sell classic portraiture. The two styles just don't work together. The style of font that you use will either draw clients or chase them away. For the high-end client looking for classical portraiture, you don't want to use comical, whimsical fonts. What you want to convey is a sense of style, grace, and class that elicits their interest in the elegance of fine portraiture. Don't hesitate to buy additional fonts and load them into Photoshop. Some of my favorite fonts are the "Artist Series" fonts, available from P22 Type Foundry, www.p22.com.

● FONT COLOR

One very important aspect of text is the color that you choose. You want

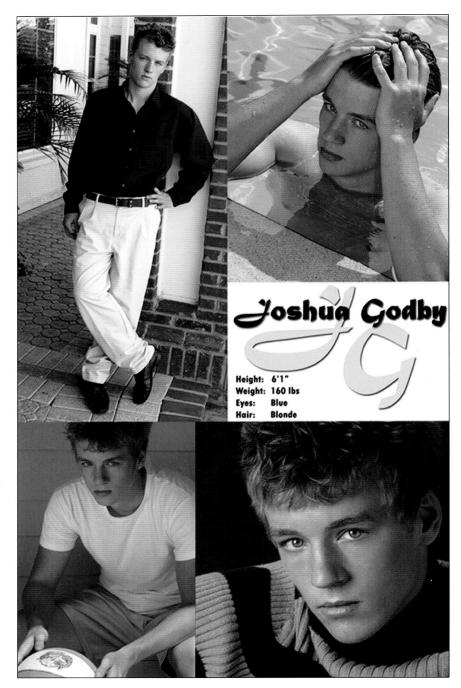

The color and style of the text you choose should match the message of the piece you are creating.

the text to be easy to read. Thus, you wouldn't want to put yellow text on a white background or dark-blue text on a black background. What you *do* want is for the color of your font to match the audience that you are targeting and the kind of emotional message you want to evoke from them. Each color has its own personality and conveys a different message to the client. Keep in mind that there are also various shades of each color that you can use. You want to grab their attention, to speak the message and covey the look that you want.

● LESS IS MORE

In many cases, it's easy to overdo it with your text. Again, don't overwhelm people. Pick your words carefully, keep them to a minimum, and, whenever possible, let your photos do the talking for you. The same is true whether you are designing a marketing piece or a digital album. In albums, it is especially important to remember that the *photographs* are the primary focus of the album; they should not be overpowered by words. Keep the text easy to read on every page, and remember that less is more.

Today I will marry my best friend

It's easy to overdo it with text, so pick your words carefully and keep the focus on the photographs.

CONSISTENCY

Keep in mind, as well, that consistency in the text used in your marketing pieces is imperative. Find a look you like for the text and stick to it. If every marketing piece you produce has a different font style, size, and color, you'll create confusion—people either won't notice that all the different pieces originated from one studio or they won't understand what your studio has to offer. Instead, develop a unified message and look in your marketing pieces, so they will be instantly recognizable as yours. This way, each marketing piece will help to reinforce your image and your message to your clients.

PHOTOSHOP TIPS FOR TEXT

1. To quickly change your fonts in Photoshop, highlight your text by clicking and dragging over it. Then, highlight the font style in the Options bar at the top of the screen. Using your up- and down-arrow keys, you can move through all of the fonts (watching as they change on your screen) to make a selection.

2. To change the font size, highlight text by clicking and dragging over it. Then, highlight the font size in the Options bar at the top of the screen. Using your up- and down-arrow keys, you can then increase or decrease the font size.

3. If you prefer not to see it, hitting Control + H hides the text highlight.

High-school seniors love to have their name added to images. For this portrait of Enesha, the image was captured on a high-key backdrop. The red square behind the subject was added in Photoshop using a layer mask. Choosing the Vertical Text tool, her name was added. Then, a black outline was put on the text by going to the Add Layer Style menu at the bottom of the Layers palette and selecting Stroke.

TEXT EFFECTS: RICK BOND, 007

In this example, text played an integral part in defining the image. Instead of text being an add-on to compliment the image, it is *part* of the image. For

Rick Bond, 007, the two images shown below were brought together in Photoshop so that my daughter, Cassie, would look like she had a twin. The instructions for the final image (shown on the next page) follow.

The original images (Rick Bond, 007).

1. Create a white background for the new image by going to File>New and selecting the size needed for the background. For this image, I set the size at 10 x 10 inches at 250 dpi).

2. For the initial text color, choose a bright orange color in the Color palette and set it as your foreground color.

3. With the Text tool selected, type the numbers "007".

4. Highlight text, then highlight the font style in the Options bar and use the up- and down-arrow keys on your keyboard to move through all of the fonts and make a selection. Here, the font used was Franklin Gothic Heavy.

5. To change the font size, highlight the text, then highlight the size field in the Options bar. Use the up- and down-arrow keys on your keyboard to increase or decrease size of your text.

6. In your Styles Folder (figure 8), with all of the Styles loaded, choose Hot Burst to achieve the text effect in this image.

7. Hit Ctrl/Cmd + J to make a copy of your text on a new layer. This duplicate layer will be used to create the shadow of the text.

8. With black set as your foreground color, go to Edit>Fill to fill the text with black.

9. With the Move tool, drag the black-filled copy of the original text into position below the original text.

10. Go to Edit>Transform>Flip Vertical to turn the text upside down.

11. Go to Edit>Transform>Flip Skew, then click and drag out the handles

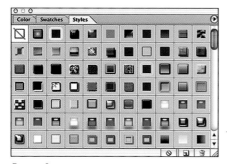

Figure 8.

of the transform box to skew the text to the side (making it look like a shadow).

12. In the Layers palette, lower the opacity of the black-text layer until you get the look of a shadow, as seen in the final image.

13. Using selections, copy the subjects from the other images into the new document.

14. Use the Clone Stamp, Healing Brush, and whatever other tools you like to seamlessly blend the subjects and do any needed retouching. In this case, for example, Cassie's knee had to be extended in one image to eliminate the pillow that her knee was resting on.

7. DIGITAL HANDCOLORING

I imagine all of us have had handed down to us a handcolored photograph of a family member from a previous generation. The handcoloring of photographs has been around almost as long as photography itself. Research shows that there are handcolored photographs dating back as early as 1842—and perhaps even earlier.

● THE HISTORY OF HANDCOLORING

Handcoloring is a classic technique, but the results can be very contemporary.

Love is a moment that lasts forever

The first handcolored photographs were tinted with fine powders that were applied very carefully with a brush. Later, they were colored with watercolor paints. Although handcolored images have, in recent years, been created using dyes, marker pens, and pencils, the most traditional technique for handcoloring is achieved by using Marshall Oils, a translucent paint applied with cotton swabs onto a print. The translucency allow the details in the image to show through, resulting in a light, subtle coloring of a photograph without the vividness of color film. Traditionally, a handcolored print was made using a black & white image printed on mat, fiber-based paper. The image was also frequently sepia toned, as this produced a base for the other colors and also produced a more pleasing background for the applied colors.

In the 1950s, with the advancement of color film, handcoloring photographs became less and less popular until, in the mid-1970s, it again emerged as a new art form. Still, however, few photographers offered handcolored images to their clients. Today, with the introduction of the computer and digital-imaging software, it has become less time-consuming to produce handcolored images. The choice to handcolor digitally is not, however, one based primarily on efficiency. Rather, digital handcoloring is the choice of many professionals because of the control it gives you over the image—allowing you to mix media, avoid harsh chemicals, and revert back to the original image if you make a mistake.

In my case, handcoloring fiber-based prints was actually what introduced me to Photoshop. A darkroom lab technician at the university where I was taking photography classes, asked me about a photograph of mine that was displayed in the university's art gallery. The image had been handcolored the traditional way with Marshall Oils. He inquired about the time it took me to apply the paint to the photograph. I told him that it depended on the print, and could take me as long as nine to twelve hours on a print. His reply was, "Do you know that

Handcoloring can also be combined with sepia toning for a very appealing look.

what takes you nine hours traditionally can be done digitally in Photoshop in thirty minutes?" That was the first time I had even *heard* of Photoshop. After spending some time researching the tools needed to work in Photoshop, I began the journey. Although the learning curve is steep, programs like Photoshop and Painter soon became an exciting new medium for my artistic expression. As it turns out, the only thing my lab-technician friend forgot to mention was that that ability to handcolor in thirty minutes would take me *three years* to learn!

● HANDCOLORING TECHNIQUES: CASSIE AND FRIENDS

My preferred method of handcoloring digitally is to use Photoshop's Brush tool in the Color and Overlay modes. This image of my daughter Cassie with her three friends is a classic example of handcoloring that would be very appealing to a high-school senior. The effect was done as follows:

1. Open the original image in Photoshop.
2. Color correct and retouch the image as needed.

Handcoloring the subjects' shirts, lips, and eyes produced a look that would be very appealing to a high-school senior.

3. Convert the image to black & white using the Lab color-conversion method as discussed in chapter 11.

4. Since the image is in the RGB mode, it will allow you to paint color back into the photograph.

5. Using the Brush tool set in the Color mode, select colors and paint them onto the image. Here, the shirts, eyes, and lips were colored.

● HANDCOLORING TECHNIQUES: JAMAICA, MON

Because the previous image is a contemporary shot, I colorized the clothing with bright colors. To make an image more representative of traditional handcoloring, let's look at the process used to create *Jamaica, Mon.*

Original image (Jamaica, Mon).

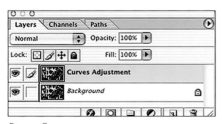

Figure 9.

1. The original image was taken in Jamaica at the local craft marketplace with black & white film, and then developed traditionally in the darkroom.

2. The negative was then scanned with a Nikon 8000 scanner. The advantage of the Nikon scanner is that it has Digital Ice, which automatically takes out any dust or scratches on the negative. This saves you hours of time in Photoshop dust spotting your negative.

3. The image was opened in Photoshop.

4. The background layer was copied by dragging in onto the Create a New Layer icon at the bottom of the Layers palette (figure 9). (For a shortcut to perform this, hit Ctrl/Cmd + J.

5. The image was adjusted using the Curves (Image>Adjustment>

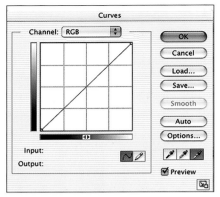

Figure 10.

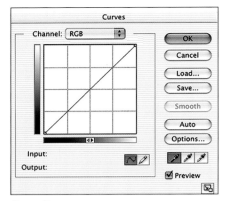

Figure 11.

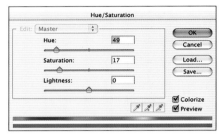

Figure 12.

Curves). In the Curves dialog box, I selected the Set White Point Eyedropper (figure 10) and clicked on the whitest part of the entire image. Then, with the Set Black Point Eyedropper, I clicked on the darkest part of the entire image (figure 11). Finally, on the Curve, I clicked in the very center of the line and dragged it up to brighten the image.

6. I merged down this layer (Layer>Merge Down).

7. I made another copy of the retouched layer by following step 4.

8. To create a custom sepia tone on the man, I went to to Image>Adjustments>Hue/Saturation (you can also press Ctrl/Cmd + U). When the Hue/Saturation dialog box popped up (figure 13), I checked the Colorize box, then used the Hue slider to select a sepia tone.

9. To take away the sepia tone on the background, I clicked on the Add a Mask icon at the bottom of the Layers palette. With my Brush tool set at 100-percent opacity, with a hard-edged brush and with black set as the foreground color, I brought back in all of the background (figure 14, previous page). (If you accidentally color on the subject while doing an operation like this, simply toggle to white as your foreground color by pressing the X key and paint over the subject to restore it.)

10. Next, I made a copy of the retouched layer by repeating step 4.

11. I then brightened the eyes with the Dodge tool and outlined the iris of the eye with the Burn tool (figure 15).

12. I exchanged the gun on the man's necklace for a circle medallion that I created in Photoshop.

13. I merged down to the retouched layer.

14. Next, I made a copy of the retouched layer (repeating step 4 again).

15. Using the Brush tool in the Color mode, I selectively colored each

Figure 13.

Figure 14.

Figure 15.

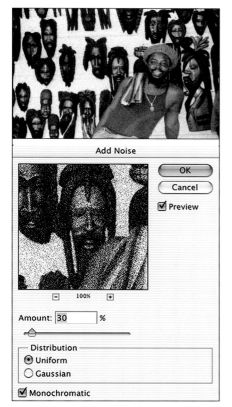

Add Noise

OK
Cancel
☑ Preview

⊟ 100% ⊞

Amount: 30 %

─ Distribution ─
⦿ Uniform
◯ Gaussian

☑ Monochromatic

Figure 16.

individual mask. I chose a low opacity for the brush, but the opacity you choose will depend on the translucency and color saturation you prefer.

16. I made another copy (see step 4) of the previous layer.

17. The Poster Edges filter was applied to this layer (Filter>Artistic>Poster Edges). The degree of the posterizing effect is a matter of preference. You can adjust it by changing the opacity of the layer in the Layers palette.

18. Another layer mask was added and the Brush tool (set at 100-percent opacity with a hard-edged brush and with black as the foreground color) was used to mask out the posterizing effect on all areas of the skin. (Again, switch the foreground color to white to restore any background areas you accidentally paint out.)

19. I made another copy of the previous layer.

20. The Noise filter was then applied (Filter>Noise>Add Noise). I clicked on Uniform Distribution and Monochromatic and set it at 30 percent (figure 16).

21. Another layer mask was added and the Brush tool (set at 100-percent opacity with a hard-edged brush and with black as the foreground color) was used to mask out the noise on all areas of the skin.

22. The final image (above) was put on a digital mat and a stroke was added around the edge using one of the colors from the mask to complement the image.

Final image.

8. POSTERIZATION

$\mathcal{P}$osterization could be discussed along with artistic filters but, because I use it so much, I wanted to give it a chapter to itself. Posterization can be a mishap or a deliberate effect applied for artistic purposes. It limits the number of colors so that the

Portraits look best when the posterization effect is minimized on the face and exposed skin. Original image (above) and final image (left).

change from one color to another is sudden rather than gradual. In Photoshop, the Posterize command (Image>Adjustments>Posterize) can be used to automate posterization but the result allows for little control over the image. My preferred method is to use the Poster Edges filter by choosing Filters>Artistic>Poster Edges.

As seen in the image of Natalie (facing page), portraits look best when the posterization effect is minimized on the face and exposed skin. In this case, I selectively eliminated it using a layer mask. With black set as the foreground color, and the Brush tool selected and set to 100-percent opacity, the effect was simply brushed away from her arms and face. Her name was added by painting it in with a graphics pen, using the Brush tool set to the Normal mode. The Bevel & Emboss layer style and a drop shadow were also added to the name by clicking on the Layer Style icon at the bottom of the Layers palette.

● POSTERIZING TECHNIQUES: A COLORFUL SENIOR PORTRAIT

Seniors today love the contemporary, colorful styles that are typical of the nontraditional portrait. This image is a great example of how a few artistic effects can dramatically alter an image and produce an "edgy" look.

Original image (A Colorful Senior Portrait).

1. Open the image and make a copy of the background.
2. Select the Gradient tool in Photoshop's Toolbar and choose a gradient from the drop-down menu in the options bar. I chose a pastel gradient from the Color Harmonies 1 folder (click on the arrow at the top right of the gradient drop-down menu to append this to your current

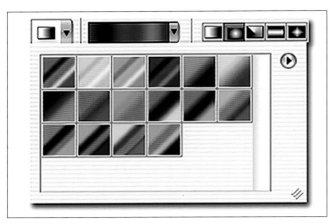

Figure 17.

Figure 18.

list of available gradients). Go to Image>Adjustments>Gradient Map
and apply the gradient of your choice (figures 17 and 18).

3. After applying the Gradient Map, I made a Curves adjustment
(Image>Adjustments>Curves) to shift the colors even more. I clicked
on the curve at several points and raised it until I achieved the look I
wanted (figures 19 and 20).

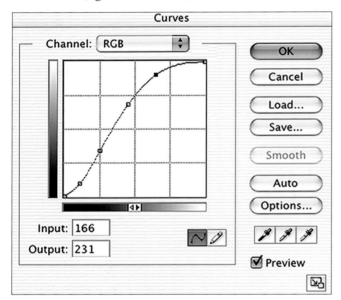

Figure 20.

Figure 19.

4. The dark-blue rectangular boxes in the background were created by
making a selection using the Rectangular Marquee tool. I then filled
the selection (Edit>Fill) with a shade of blue sampled from the jacket
using the Eyedropper tool (which sets the color you click on as the
foreground color).

5. The additional graphics were achieved by making selections with the
Rectangular Marquee tool, then adding a stroke to the active selec-

Final image.

Original image (Senior Portrait
with a Background Effect).

tion (Edit>Stroke). Where the resulting lines ran over the subject, a layer mask was used to eliminate them.

6. The final step was to posterize the image by choosing Filters>Artistic>Poster Edges.

● POSTERIZING TECHNIQUES: SENIOR PORTRAIT WITH A BACKGROUND EFFECT

1. Open a color-corrected, retouched portrait (left).
2. Go to Filter>Artistic>Poster Edges and apply the filter.
3. Click on the Add a Mask icon at the bottom of the Layers palette.
4. With black set as your foreground color, use the Brush tool at 100-percent opacity to mask out the effect of the filter and let the senior show through.
5. Should you make a mistake, change your foreground color to white to restore the filter's effect.
6. Flatten the image.
7. To add the background, use the Rectangular Marquee tool to select an area of the wall from the flattened image.
8. Hit Ctrl/Cmd + J to place the selected area on its own layer.

9. Go to File>New to create a blank white document the size desired for the background (the size needed will be determined by the size of the print you intend to make; here it was a 16 x 20).

10. With the Move tool, drag the selection of the wall over into the white document.

11. Press Ctrl/Cmd + T to Free Transform the image and, holding down the Shift key, drag out the diagonal arrows to increase the size of the selection to fit over the entire white background. Flatten the image.

12. With the Move tool, drag the image of the senior over onto the new background.

13. Hit Ctrl/Cmd) + T to Free Transform the image. With the turn arrows, rotate the image to a diagonal position.

14. Click on the Add Layer Style icon at the bottom of the Layers palette and select Stroke to add a black outline to the edge of the image.

Final image.

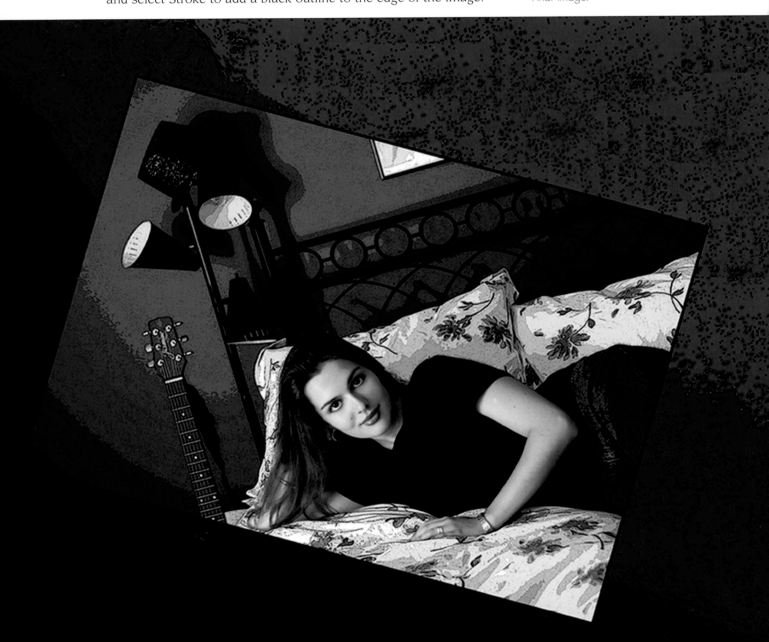

● POSTERIZING TECHNIQUES: CD COVER

1. Open a retouched image.

2. Ctrl/Cmd + J to make a copy of the image.

3. Go to Filter>Artistic>Poster Edges to posterize the image (figure 21).

Original image.

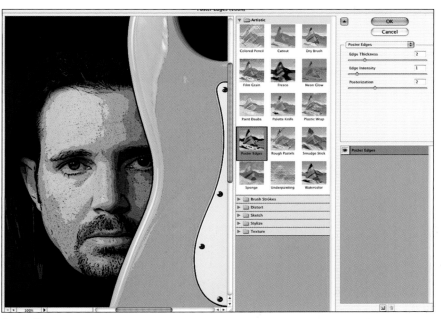

Figure 21

4. Add a mask by clicking on the Add a Mask icon at the bottom of the Layers palette.

5. With black as the foreground color, use the Brush tool to mask out any unwanted posterization.

6. Flatten the image.

7. Go to File>New to create a new document for the background, making it five inches taller and wider than the portrait.

8. With the Eyedropper tool, select a color from the image (in this case, it was the guitar) for your foreground color.

9. Fill the new document with the new color by going to Edit>Fill and choosing Foreground Color from the Use pull-down menu.

10. Using the Move tool, drag your portrait into the new image window. Holding the Shift key as you drag the image will allow you to perfectly center it over the new background.

11. To add a black stroke to the image, click on the Add Layer Style icon at the bottom of the Layers palette and choose Stroke. Change the default color from red to black, then choose Inside Stroke.

12. Using the Text tool, add whatever text you like to the bottom of the CD cover.

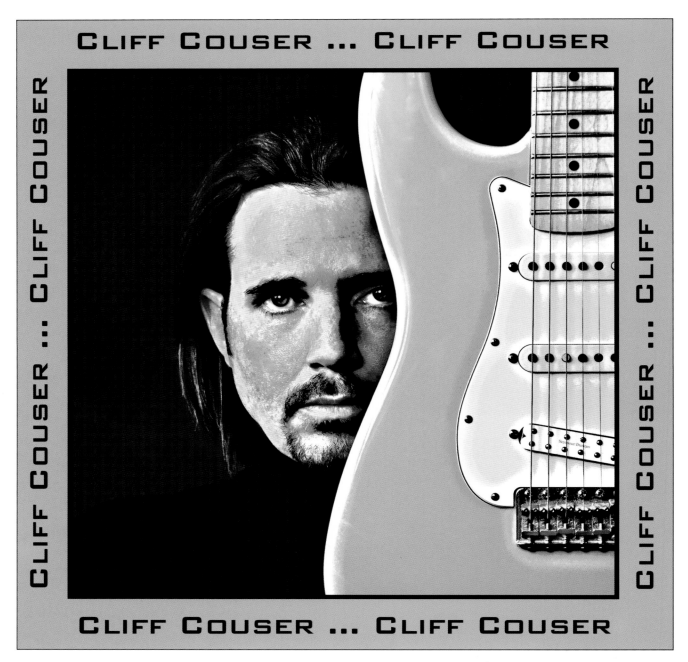

Final image.

13. Hit Ctrl/Cmd + J to make a copy of the text.

14. With the Move tool, reposition the copy of the first text to the top of the CD cover.

15. Turn the document on its side by going to Image>Rotate>90 Degrees Clockwise.

16. Repeat steps 14 through 16.

17. Turn the document so that it is correctly oriented, then flatten the image.

9. CREATIVE CLONING

*C*loning is merely transferring pixels from one part of the image to another. You can even paint on a blank document and transfer information by painting it in with the Clone tool (in Photoshop) or Cloner Brushes (in Painter). Cloning can be considered comparable to collaging that is done traditionally.

With Painter, cloning becomes an adventure with a myriad of possibilities for creating a work of art, because the Cloner brushes allow you to apply the textures and effects of a variety of brush applications without the addition of color. This allows you to turn a photo into a painting without changing its color palette—and without any ability to draw or paint from scratch. As simple as it is, this technique surpasses the simple application of plug-in filters by allowing you to create art that no one can duplicate.

● CLONING TECHNIQUES: IMPRESSIONIST LANDSCAPE

This image of a French countryside is a beautiful landscape just as a straight photographic print. Using a simple cloning technique in Painter, however, allowed me to turn it into a beautiful art piece in something like the Impressionist style of the French artist Monet.

Original image (Impressionist Landscape).

1. The original image was brought into Painter and cloned by going to File>Clone.
2. The image was then selected by choosing Select>All.
3. The tracing paper was activated by clicking on the Toggle Tracing Paper box at the top-right corner of the cloned image. Checking this box turns on tracing paper and the original image is seen under a low opacity paper.
4. I then used the Impressionistic variant of the Cloner brushes to clone in the original image, giving it an artistic look.

Final image.

5. As I worked on the image, I also added additional color in the sky and on the buildings using a combination of the Chalk and Oil brushes, returning back to the Impressionistic variant of the Cloner brushes to achieve the finished result.

As you can see, the image that has been "painted" evokes more warmth and emotion than the original photograph (shown on the previous page). The increased saturation of the colors, the dabbing of the brush strokes, and the increased detail in the buildings all enhance the image and bring life to the painting.

● **CLONING TECHNIQUES: FLORAL IMPRESSION**

Several Painter techniques were use to create *Floral Impression.*

1. Before bringing the original photograph into Painter, open the image in Photoshop and add a white border around it. To do this, select white as your background color in the Toolbar, then go to Image>Canvas Size. When the window opens, increase your canvas size by four inches in both the height and width (figure 22). By increasing the canvas size, you will create enough extra room to paint out from the edges of the original photograph (figure 23).

2. Open the photograph (with the increased canvas size) in Painter and make a clone of it by going to File>Clone.

3. Go to Select>All, then hit Delete. When you do this, a white canvas will appear to cover the photograph. Activate the Toggle Tracing Paper icon in the top-right corner of the window, however, and the

Original image (Floral Impression).

Figure 22.

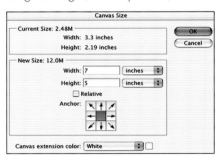
Figure 23.

Figure 24.

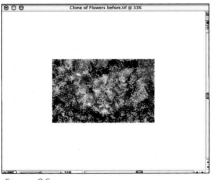

Figure 25.

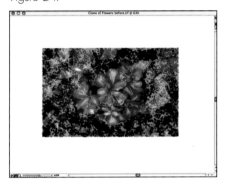

Figure 26.

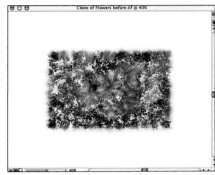

Figure 27.

image will appear immediately from underneath the white canvas (figure 24).

4. In the Cloner brushes, choose the variant called Texture Spray. Make the size 27.4 and set the opacity to 100 percent. Gently tap the graphics pen over the tracing paper to reveal a light spray of the original photograph (figure 25).

5. Choose an additional variant from the Cloner brushes called Smeary Bristle. Set its size to 52.2 and its opacity to 100 percent. Smear and clone in the pink flower in the center of the image (figure 26).

6. Choose the Cloner brush variant called Flat Impasto Cloner. Set its size to 15.6 and its opacity to 72 percent. Use the brush to bring back detail in the image.

7. Choose the Soft Cloner variant set at 137.6 and 9-percent opacity and lightly go over the image to bring back a hint of the original photo.

8. At this point, you will change from the Cloner brushes to the Blender brushes. Choosing the Grainy Blender 30 Variant set at 20-percent opacity, the surrounding edge of the photograph was blended into the white border, removing any hard lines (figure 27, previous page).

9. White was added back to the center flowers by selecting the Chalk brushes and picking the Square Chalk variant at a size of 21.5 and at 100-percent opacity with white selected. Dark red was also applied to the center of the flowers using the same variant and method.

10. Switch back to the Blender brushes and choose the Grainy Blender 10 variant at 15-percent opacity to blend the paint of the flowers where the color was added.

11. The last step in Painter is to choose the Flat Impasto Cloner variant from the Cloner brushes at a size of 15.6 and 72-percent opacity to bring back additional detail to the center flowers.

12. The Painter image was saved as a TIFF file and opened in Photoshop to add contrast and depth to the color. Make a copy of the back-

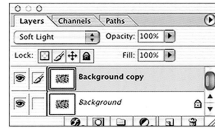

Figure 28 (above) and final image (left).

Original image (Flower Power).

ground and change the blending mode (in the Layers palette) to Soft Light (figure 28) for the final result (above).

● CLONING TECHNIQUES: FLOWER POWER

This image was made from a scanned transparency of flowers. The original image appears to the right.

Figure 29.

1. Working in Photoshop, the first effect was to increase the color saturation by going to Image>Adjustments>Hue/Saturation.
2. Next, I added a watercolor effect (Filter>Artistic>Dry Brush) (figure 29).
3. The image was then cropped to cut off some of the blue flowers and green leaves
4. Holding down the Shift key to center the image, the Move tool was used to transfer the image to a new image file window with a black background that was larger than the flowers (figure 30).
5. The pink stroke was added by going to the Add Layer Style icon at the bottom of the Layers palette and choosing Stroke.
6. The default color of the stroke was changed by using the Eyedropper tool and selecting a shade of pink from the flowers.
7. I then went back to the original cropped image and stepped back in the History palette to the state prior to cropping the image.
8. A variety of blue flowers and leaves were selected (one at a time) using the Lasso tool.
9. The individual flowers and leaves were put on their own layers by typing Ctrl/Cmd + J.

Figure 30.

Final image (Flower Power).

Original image (Wrapped in Flowers).

10. Each selection was moved one at a time to the flower image on the black background to overlap the pink stroke.

11. Each flower and leaf was turned and moved as needed using the Free Transform command (Ctrl + T).

● CLONING TECHNIQUES: WRAPPED IN FLOWERS

I was in a vintage store and found a beautiful flowered hat from the 1960s. Immediately, I thought of an artistic image. At the end of a bridal portrait session, I asked the bride if she would pose for me in the flowered hat. I had her lay down on a posing table and quickly snapped the shutter to get a base image for what I planned to create in Photoshop. As you can see from the original image (below left), the lighting is not what it needs to be, but I knew that I was going to change all of that in the final image.

As shown in the instructions below, the image was "glamour retouched" (see chapter 16 for more on this) and the flowers from the hat were cloned around the subject to create this beautiful image titled *Wrapped in Flowers*.

1. After opening the image, the flowers were wrapped around the bottom left of the image using the Clone tool at 100-percent opacity.

2. The next step was to select specific roses from the hat using the Lasso tool.

3. With a rose selected, hit Ctrl/Cmd + J to jump the selected rose to its own layer.

4. With your Move tool, drag the rose into a new position, transforming or rotating it as desired to create an organic look.

5. The next step was to add a mask by going to the Add a Mask icon at the bottom of your Layers palette.

6. With black set as the foreground color, mask out any of the rose that does not fit as you wish.

7. Merge down your layer.

8. The subject's lipstick was then matched to the color of one of the roses by using the Eyedropper tool to select a specific color.

9. Using the Brush tool in the Color mode, the lips were then painted with the selected color.

Final image.

Photoshop makes it easy to create beautiful collages.

W hile Photoshop *does* allow you to paint and create artistic designs, the blending and spreading from one color to another cannot be accomplished as well as in Painter. This is because the tools in Painter are specifically designed to function like actual brushes used by artists; those in Photoshop are not.

Grace

When it comes to combining elements from various images, however, Photoshop is the tool of choice. For example, a lot of my inspiration for my pieces comes from my travel throughout the world—from the architecture, landscapes, and artifacts of art that I see around me. Often, though, I see an object that inspires me, and although I photograph it, I realize that something is missing from the image. This is the point at which I turn to Photoshop and begin adding elements from other images. As the image grows, it takes on a life of its own. It's only after doing this that the finished product results.

Don't be afraid to experiment with different layouts and designs. As the image evolves, you'll find it takes on a life of its own.

The newest product in wedding albums is the digitally designed album.

While compositing is an excellent technique for creating fine-art images, it has also come to be used widely by professional photographers in album design. In fact, the newest product in wedding albums is the digitally designed album. Unlike traditional albums, digital albums allow you to easily incorporate text and color mats. You can also overlay images to increase the number of photographs displayed on a single page. It is a beautiful way to artistically tell the story of your clients' romance and their special day, giving your album a personal touch as individual as your photography.

As you'll notice throughout the examples that follow, anytime you are combining multiple images, the layer mask will become your new best friend. It allows for mistakes to be corrected, so you can retrieve the original information when needed. If you are not comfortable working with layer masks, experiment with them and refer to a basic Photoshop manual to answer any questions you might have.

● COLLAGE TECHNIQUES: INNOCENT CHILD

To create this composite, I used four separate images. The baby's father's hand was photographed in a cupped position, keeping the concept of the final design in mind. Next, the baby was photographed in position on a pillow. Because we could not get the baby's head to look toward the camera while in that position, we had to take the baby's face from a different pose. The wings were photographed separately and reduced in size in Photoshop using the Free Transform tool. Finally, the images were brought together, starting with the father's hand as the background image.

1. I began by creating a new document (File>New) with a white background, set to the size of the final image.
2. Next, I opened the image of the father's hand (figure 31) and resized it (Image>Adjustments>Image Size) to match the size of the white document.
3. I chose the Move tool and, while holding down the Shift key, dragged the image of the father's hand over to the newly created white document (figure 32).
4. I lowered the opacity of the new layer (the image of the father's hand) in the Layers palette, resulting in a dreamy, heavenly appearance (figure 33).
5. Next, I merged down the two layers to create an original background.
6. I made a copy of the background layer by dragging the background to

Figure 31.

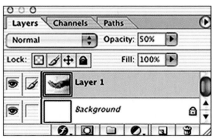
Figure 32.

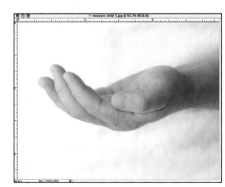
Figure 33.

the Create a New Layer icon at the bottom of the Layers palette. (For a shortcut to perform this, hit Ctrl/Cmd + J.)

7. I opened up the image of the baby and made a loose selection of the baby's body using the Lasso tool (figure 34), then dragged it over to the background (figure 35).

Figure 34.

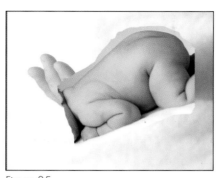

Figure 35.

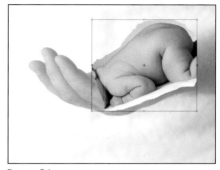

Figure 36.

8. The next step was to resize (Edit>Transform>Scale) the baby's body and position it in the father's hand (figure 36).

9. I added a layer mask by clicking on the Add a Mask icon in the bottom of the Layers palette. Then, with my Brush tool set at 100-percent opacity, I chose a hard-edged brush and set the foreground color to black. Using this, I masked out the background around the baby's body. If part of the baby's body was accidentally masked out, I toggled to white as the foreground color and restored it. I then merged down to the copy of my background.

10. I repeated the same process (steps 7, 8, and 9) with the baby's head (figure 37) and the angel wings (figure 38).

Figure 37.

Figure 38.

11. To complete the image, I flattened it, converted it to black & white, and added text.

Behold the wonder of an innocent child...

for such is the kingdom of Heaven

Final image.

● COLLAGE TECHNIQUES: RAVINES COMMERCIAL COLLAGE

1. When creating a collage, open all the images you wish to use for the collage, making sure that the size and resolution of each is the same.

2. Create a new background by going to File>New and determine the size of your collage.

3. Choose the Crop tool and click on the Clear box in the Options bar to remove all the previous settings. Then, crop each image as desired.

4. With the Move tool, drag each photograph onto the background image. You can free transform each image (Edit>Free Transform) to change it to the desired size.

5. With the Auto Select Layer activated in the Move tool options, drag each image to the desired placement.

6. To overlap the images, click and drag on the various layers in the Layers palette to rearrange them as you like.

7. Once the images are in the desired positions, create a drop shadow for the image at the top of the Layers palette. To do this, click on the layer to activate it. Then, go to the Add Layer Style icon at the bottom of the Layers palette and choose Drop Shadow (figure 39).

8. The next step was to drag this Drop Shadow layer style from the first layer to each of the layers beneath to apply the same effect to each.

9. Text was then added to complete the collage (facing page).

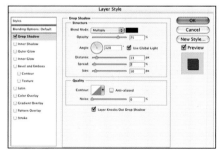

Figure 39.

Final image (facing page).

RavineS

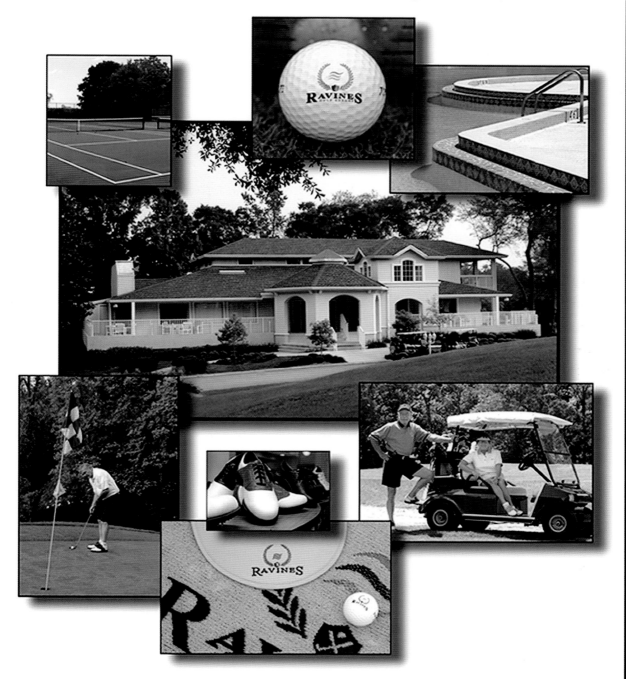

Images By Signature Studio   www.rickferro.com   904.288.6464

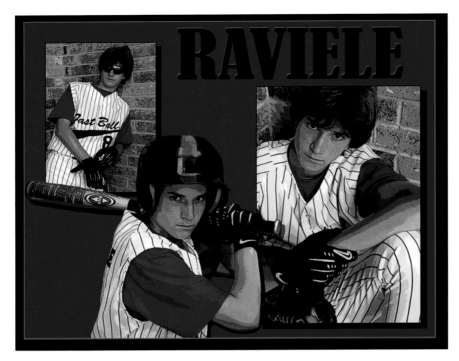

● COLLAGE TECHNIQUES: SENIOR PORTRAIT

1. To create this image, I began by opening three color-corrected images.

2. Then I followed the steps found on pages 47–48 for adding a Poster Edges effect, making sure to mask out any unwanted effects on the face.

3. Following the directions on page 62 for the Ravines commercial collage, I created a new image file of the desired size with a red background. Then, I added the inset images that appear on the upper left and lower right in the final composite.

4. To create the cut-out image of the senior in his baseball uniform, I used the Lasso tool to loosely select the senior in the original image.

5. Then, I hit Ctrl/Cmd + J to put the selection on its own layer.

6. With the Move tool, I dragged the new layer (the senior) over onto the background and positioned it at the lower left. To ensure that this image overlaid the other two images, I placed it at the top of the Layers palette.

7. Next, I clicked on the Add a Mask icon at the bottom of the Layers palette to create a mask.

8. With Black as the foreground color, I used the Brush tool set at 100-percent opacity to mask out any unwanted edges around the player (changing back to white as the foreground color to restore the subject if I masked out too much).

9. Then, I flattened the image and added text.

10. Finally, I put the final image on a black background and added a blue stroke around the red background.

● COLLAGE TECHNIQUES: THE THREE FACES OF CASSIE

This collage is based on a technique that I learned from Larry Peters. To accomplish it, you need to intentionally overexpose each image when you shoot it. For these images, the main light and the background light were set to f/16 while the camera was set at f/8. You know that you have overexposed enough when you can just see the tip of the subject's nose and very little other detail on the skin. This makes for a beautiful white-on-white glamour portrait. Here, three separate images of Cassie were loosely selected with the Lasso tool and brought over into a white document. Using a layer mask, I erased the edges of the selection that obstructed any of the other images. Placing the images on a diagonal through the rectangular frame created a pleasing composition, which was completed by the addition of two black strokes.

Final image
(Three Faces of Cassie).

● COLLAGE TECHNIQUES: IN SEARCH OF HERSELF

Three images were brought together in Photoshop to make the collage titled, *In Search of Herself*. By lowering the opacity of the layer of the image where Cassie is facing the backdrop, I made it look like a mirror image of her. Notice that, in the final image, two portraits of Cassie were combined

Original images (left).

Final image (below).

to create the primary image of her (the one where she is facing the camera). I used the face and upper torso from one shot and the arms and lower body from another to create the look I wanted.

● COLLAGE TECHNIQUES: HIGH-KEY SENIOR COLLAGE

Thanks to another technique I learned from a class with Larry Peters, I started offering this type of collage for my high-school seniors. For this image, I photographed Rachel in the same spot on a high-key background but in different poses. By keeping her in the same spot, I was able to loosely select her in Photoshop with the Lasso tool and combine the images. It's a great artistic design that is easy to sell to high-school seniors. The instructions for this image are as follows.

1. Open several images from a senior session. The images need to be captured on the same background, with the same lighting, with the subject in the same position, and at the same camera angle. Five to seven images works best when doing this collage.
2. With the Lasso tool, loosely select around each subject, feathering your selection by two pixels.
3. Create a new document the size of your finished collage and at the resolution you need for output.
4. With the Move tool activated, drag each selection from the various images over into the new document (figure 40). (It is most convenient to have the seniors the same size you need and at the same resolution of the background so that they will easily fit within the new document. If you need to scale them, however, go to Edit>Transform> Scale and hold down the Shift key while adjusting the scale; this will maintain the proper aspect ratio, so your subject won't look stretched or distorted.)
5. You can add a layer mask to any of the image layers to clean up any area of your loose selection that might overlap another image. To add a layer mask, click on the Add a Mask icon at the bottom of the Layers palette. With black set as your foreground color and your Brush tool set at a 100-percent opacity, mask out any part of your layer that overlaps another image. (Remember that switching to white as the foreground color

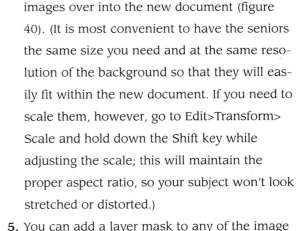

Figure 40.

will allow you to restore any
areas you accidentally mask out.)

Figure 41.

6. Activate the background layer at
the bottom of your Layers palette
by clicking on it.

7. Make a rectangular selection by
clicking and dragging your
Rectangular Marquee tool down
and across the left side of the image. To create the second rectangle,
hold down the Shift key and drag horizontally across the bottom of
the image (figure 41).

8. With the Eyedropper tool, select a shade of pink from the subject's
dress. This fills your foreground color box with pink.

9. Fill your selections with pink by going to Edit>Fill>Foreground Color
(figure 42).

10. Ctrl/Cmd + D to deselect the pink boxes (figure 43).

11. Activate the Text tool and choose a font for the name. In this illustra-
tion, a single font was used to type in the name, but the "R" was
placed on one text layer, and the rest of the name was placed on

Figure 42.

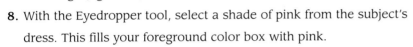

Figure 43.

Final image.

another. The "R" was then set at a much larger size than the rest of the name.

12. After rasterizing the type, a layer mask was added to erase any of the text that overlapped the subject.

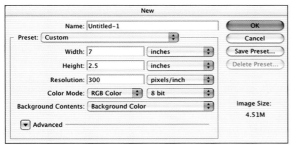

● COLLAGE TECHNIQUES: THE FUJI FILMSTRIP

You can create your own filmstrip by scanning one or you can create it in Photoshop. The one shown here was created in Photoshop and is 7 inches wide by 2.5 inches high. If you save this template as an unflattened PSD file, you will be able to copy and paste images into it as needed. To make a longer filmstrip, just string several copies of this template together.

Figure 44.

Figure 45.

1. Make black your background color in Photoshop.
2. Go to File>New.
3. Enter the dimensions (7 x 2.5 inches) for the template and the resolution needed for your lab or printer—and double-check that the Background Contents is set to background color! (figure 44).
4. Go to View>Show>Grid. (You can change your grid's dimensions by going to Edit>Preferences>Guides, Grid & Slices.)
5. Next, create the white squares that will hold your images.
6. Go to File>New and create a new document that is 2 x 2 inches and matches the resolution you selected for the image created in step 3. Make sure you set the Background Contents to white.
7. Next, you need to move the 2 x 2-inch square over onto your black background to create the basic element of your filmstrip (figure 45).

To do this, activate the Move tool and hold down your Shift key while dragging the white square onto the black background. This will center the white square in the middle of the black background.

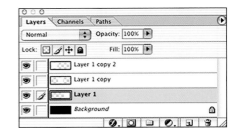

Figure 46.

8. In your Layers palette, make a copy of the white square by dragging the layer on which it appears down onto the Create a New Layer icon at the bottom of the palette. Now repeat this step, so that you end up with a total of three white squares. (You will not see the white squares right away because they will be on top of each other.)

9. With your Move tool activated, drag each square to the position on the grid to make them equal distances apart (figure 47).

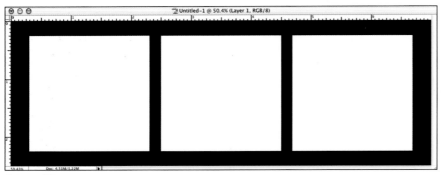

Figure 47.

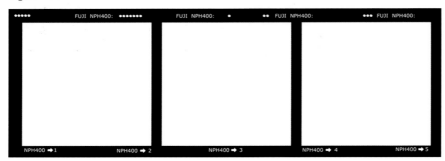

Figure 48.

10. You can now add text to your document in white or gold, stating the image number and film used. Make sure that you keep your text in layers in case you combine filmstrips and want to add additional image numbers (figure 48).

11. Save your filmstrip as a PSD file without flattening the layers. You may wish to label it "filmstrip template" or "empty filmstrip" to remind yourself that it doesn't contain images.

12. Open three images that you would like to put in your filmstrip. Crop them to 2 x 2 inches at the same resolution as your filmstrip.

13. To copy and paste your images into the filmstrip, select the Magic Wand tool and click on the first white square in your Layers palette to select it.

14. Go to the image that you want to put into the filmstrip and hold Ctrl/Cmd + A to select the image and Ctrl/Cmd + C to copy it. Return to the filmstrip (you will see that your white square is still selected), and go to Edit>Paste Into. Like magic, your image will now reside in the white square. At this point, you can resize your image by going to Free Transform (Ctrl/Cmd+ T).

15. Repeat steps 12–14 until all the white squares have been filled.

16. As long as you have saved your filmstrip prior to placing the images into it, you can now flatten the image and go to File>Save As, to save it as a TIF or JPG.

Final image (The Fuji Filmstrip).

11. COLOR WOW

*E*very color speaks a different language to your clients. Therefore, the use of color can dramatically affect the design of an image as well as the impact it has on the viewer. The color solution you decide on, and the combination of colors you use, can communicate a message that will psychologically affect the viewer, so it is important.

● COLOR ASSOCIATIONS

Red will be the first to get attention and is associated with love (a red rose), excitement, passion (think of the expression "seeing red"), adventure, and danger. Blue tends to call to mind success, genuineness, calm, power, and professionalism. Think of the calming blue ocean—or the impact of "dressing for success" in a dark blue suit ("trustworthiness") a bright red tie ("power").

Green is associated with nature, money, health, healing, and life. Orange tends to suggest creativity, youth, celebration, fun, and affordability. Purple is associated with royalty, luxury, justice, dreams, and fantasy. Yellow reminds us of happiness, cheerfulness, curiosity,

Black is associated with darkness, mystery, secrecy, and darkness.

and amusement. If you have ever photographed a wedding, you understand the significance of white, which is associated with innocence and purity. It also, however, suggests cleanliness and simplicity.

Black is associated with darkness, mystery, secrecy, and darkness. It is also associated with power. Pink can be associated with softness, tenderness, sweetness, innocence, and youthfulness. Brown is associated with nature, the earth, tribalism, simplicity, and primitive motifs. Gray is usually associated with indifference, reservation, and neutrality.

● PRIMARY COLORS

The ability to understand and use color effectively to enhance rather than distract from the design is important. Having a good understanding of primary colors and the color wheel (and how it works) is important when selecting and using colors. Each and every color has its own buddy—its "mate," if you will. These two colors, located directly across each other on the color wheel, are called complementary. When used next to each other, they become more intense.

Another effective color concept is to use four colors that are spaced equally apart on the color wheel. This produces a beautifully balanced color palette consisting of two sets of complementary colors and two related pairs of color.

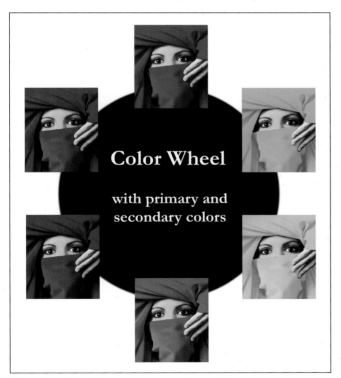

The color wheel shows primary and secondary colors.

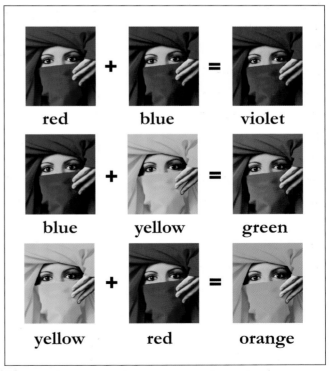

Primary colors are mixed to create secondary colors.

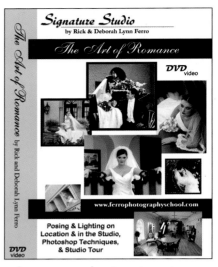

In the DVD jacket for our teaching tape called *The Art of Romance* I used complementary colors to cause the viewer's eye to move between the images long enough to read the text. This vibrancy excites the viewer and causes them to look further. Notice that when the same DVD design is produced in two shades of the same color, the impact is reduced. In the third example, the jacket is shown in black & white, causing the viewer to be lost between the text and images; it doesn't grab for attention.

This image shows how the use of primary colors can make an image stand out

Using complementary colors (blue and orange) helped show the sisters, Sydne and Bailey, as individuals—while still preserving the message about their close relationship.

Original image (French Woman).

● COLOR TECHNIQUES: THE FRENCH WOMAN

A color that evokes playfulness and cheerfulness is yellow. In this image, titled *The French Woman*, a yellow filter was applied through Layers Styles.

1. To create this portrait, I opened two images in Photoshop, one of a woman and one of flowers.
2. Next, I added a soft effect to the flower image by going to Filter>Blur>Gaussian Blur.
3. I made the flower image the size I needed for the overall image (Image>Image Size); it will be used for the background.
4. Using the Burn tool in Photoshop, I accentuated the original portrait subject's makeup and mole.
5. The next step was to cut the subject out of the portrait by loosely selecting her with the Lasso tool.
6. I then hit Ctrl/Cmd + J to put the selection on its own layer.
7. With the Move tool, I dragged the selected cut-out of the subject onto the flower background.
8. Next, I added a mask by clicking on the Add a Mask icon at the bottom of the Layers palette.
9. With black set as the foreground color, I used the Brush tool to mask out any unwanted part of the subject.
10. Using a small brush, I carefully erased areas of the straw hat to reveal the flower image behind it.
11. Next, I merged the two images by going to the pull-down menu at the top right of the Layers palette and choosing Merge Down.
12. I then hit Ctrl/Cmd + J to make a copy of the image.
13. Next, I went to the Styles palette (Window>Styles) and chose Overlay with Gold. If this style does not appear on your current list, click on the

Figure 49.

drop-down menu at the top-right of the Styles palette and select Load Styles (figure 49, previous page).

14. I made the effect of the overlay more subtle by reducing the opacity of the layer in the Layers palette.

15. Finally, I flattened the image.

In looking at the before and after versions of this image (shown on the previous page and to the left), you can see how dramatic color can contribute to a very powerful presentation.

There are several ways to selectively color an image, but the method I prefer is color masking. In the before image of Amy (above left)), I colorized the background in red using the Red style from the Styles palette (as illustrated in the above instructions for *The French Woman*). I then added a layer mask to remove the red from Amy's hair, face, and clothing as seen in the final image (above).

⊙ **COLOR TECHNIQUES: COMBINING BLACK & WHITE AND COLOR**

The following Photoshop instructions are techniques for adding color or converting to black & white.

Black & White Conversion Through Lab Color

1. Open a color-corrected image in Photoshop.
2. Go to Image>Mode>Lab Color.
3. Go to the Channels palette (Window>Channels).
4. In the Channels palette, click on the Lightness channel. This will turn your image into a black & white (figure 50).

Figure 50 (below) and final image converted to black & white using the Lab color method (right).

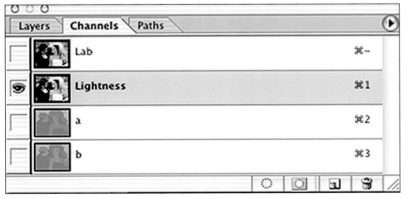

5. Go to Image>Mode>Grayscale.

6. Go to Image>Mode>RGB.

7. If necessary, adjust the contrast of the image using the Levels command (Image>Adjustments>Levels) or another tool of your choice.

Black & White and Color Combined

1. Open a color image in Photoshop (figure 51).

2. Drag the background layer onto the Create a New Layer icon at the bottom of the Layers palette to make a copy of it (figure 52).

3. Go to Image>Adjustments> Desaturate (figure 53).

4. Click on the Add a Mask icon at the bottom of the Layers palette.

5. With black set as your foreground color, use your Brush tool at 100-percent opacity to mask out any areas of the black & white image where you want to restore the color.

6. Should you make a mistake, change your foreground color to white and use it to restore the black & white image.

7. When you have reached your desired result, flatten the image.

Figure 51.

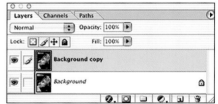

Figure 52.

Figure 53.

Final image.

In this image of a mother and child (left), black & white and color were combined to produce a strong emotional impact. Because the mother is in black & white with only a slight hint of color, it is suggested that she takes a secondary role to the child. The child, represented in color, shows the exuberance that a young one brings into the world. The use of color here helps to depict the relationship between the pair.

● COLOR TECHNIQUES:
COMBINING SEPIA AND COLOR

1. Open a color image in Photoshop.

2. Drag the image onto the Create a New Layer icon at the bottom of the Layers palette to make a copy of it.

3. In your Styles palette (Window>Styles) click on Sepia Tone. (Alternately, you can use the custom sepia-tone technique described below.)

4. Lower the opacity of the layer to soften the sepia-tone effect.

5. Click on the Add a Mask icon at the bottom of the Layers palette to add a mask.

6. With black set as your foreground color, use your Brush tool at 100-percent opacity to mask out any areas of the sepia image where you want to restore the color.

7. Should you make a mistake, change your foreground color to white and paint it on to return to the sepia image.

8. When you are done, flatten the image.

Combining sepia and color can produce an elegant image.

Custom Sepia

If you don't like the sepia tone created using the Style palette, you can create a custom sepia tone using the following procedure. To use this method when combining sepia and color, simply replace step 3 in the previous technique with steps 2–6 below.

1. Open an image in Photoshop.
2. Go to Image>Adjustments>Hue/Saturation.
3. Check the Colorize box at the bottom-right corner of the dialog box that appears (figure 54).

This is just another example of a beautiful portrait customized using sepia and color in combination.

Figure 54.

Original image for custom sepia effect (above) and final image (right).

4. Adjust the Hue slider to 38.

5. Adjust the Saturation slider to 26.

6. If you like, refine the settings of the sliders until you get just the look you want.

● COLOR TECHNIQUES: INCREASED COLOR SATURATION

1. Open a color image in Photoshop.

2. Click on the Create a New Fill or Adjustment Layer icon at the bottom of the Layers palette and choose Hue/Saturation.

3. Increase the Saturation to give desired effect to make the colors
   punch, ignoring the color shift.

4. Add a layer mask by clicking on the Add a Mask icon at the bottom
   of the Layers palette.

5. With black as your foreground color, use the Brush tool to remove
   any unwanted saturation from the image (switch to white as the
   foreground color if you make a mistake and need to restore the
   saturation in any area).

6. Flatten the image.

In these images, the saturation was increased using the described Hue/Saturation method. The image on the right, titled *The Gate*, was also brought into Painter to add additional color effects.

● **COLOR TECHNIQUES: COLOR FOR PUNCH!**

To make this image more interesting, I decided to add color to the building
for impact.

1. In Photoshop, I began by opening the image I wanted to work on.

2. I hit Ctrl/Cmd + J to create a duplicate of the image on a new layer.

3. In the Styles palette (Window>Styles) I clicked on Purple Tone.

4. Next, I added a layer mask by clicking on the Add a Mask icon at the bottom of the Layers palette.

5. With black as my foreground color, I used the Brush tool set at 100-percent opacity to add back the original colors on the subject.

6. If I made a mistake, I zoomed in and changed to white as my foreground color to add back the purple color.

7. When I had completed the coloration, I flattened the image.

Final image (Color for Punch!).

12. ARTISTIC FILTERS

$\mathcal{W}$hen you were first learning Photoshop, one of the most instantly rewarding creative tools at your disposal was probably the artistic filters. The ability to create an artistic design from a photograph with one click of the mouse is a lot of fun. However, I have found that the best results, when it comes to filters, are actually achieved when you apply multiple filters. This allows you to vary their affect through

In this image of the Eiffel Tower (left), I used the Magic Wand to select areas of the sky and grass and then increase the saturation or change the color. Then, the Dry Brush filter was applied. The image titled *Blooming Branches* (right) is another example of using the Dry Brush filter to create a watercolor effect.

This image, called *Sandy Toes*, was originally captured on film using a Hasselblad camera. It was then scanned into Photoshop using a Nikon 8000 scanner for medium-format film. The flowers were brought into the design from another image. The colors were increased in saturation and the Dry Brush filter was applied to achieve a watercolor effect. An artistic edge was applied by using Extensis Photo Frames (for more on this software, see www.extensis.com). The image was then moved to a white document and printed out on Epson Watercolor Paper.

blending modes, assuring that the artistic affect you achieve is customized rather than computerized.

When trying out different filters, it is a good idea to try each one on the same image to see its affect, always working on a layer. You can reduce its affect by lowering the opacity of the layer, or by choosing Edit>Fade Filter. With Photoshop, you can view the filters in a window called the Filter Gallery, where you can see each effect on your image before leaving the window or applying the filter. This is a huge time-saver. Remember that most filters have variable settings, so you can customize the effect produced. The possibilities are left to your imagination.

One of my favorite books for artistic design is the *The Photoshop CS Wow! Book* by Jack Davis (Peachpit Press, 2005). In it, he shows you the basic effect each filter is supposed to produce. This makes for a great hands-on guide when first learning how to use filters.

In the following sections, you'll see how I use some of *my* favorite filters. Give them a try—either alone or in combination.

● FILTER TECHNIQUES: DRY BRUSH FILTER

Because of my experience using watercolors, I was excited to apply the Watercolor filter to my photographs. However, I found that the Dry Bush filter (Filter>Artistic>Dry Brush) actually gives a truer representation of watercolor painting than the Watercolor filter (Filter>Artistic>Watercolor).

Original image (above) and final image (top).

For the image called *Bed of Roses* (next page), the subject wore a green, form-fitting dress to which silk ivy and roses were attached. We then wrapped a rose-garden garland around her. In Photoshop, creative cloning was used to add hair and flowers around the face. Glamour retouching was applied to the face and skin (see chapter 16). Finally, the Dry Brush filter was applied. To make the filter apply to just the roses and not the entire image, a layer mask was added. With black set as the foreground color, the effect of the filter was masked out from the rest of the photograph. When using any of the artistic filters on a portrait, you want to make sure that you significantly decrease or even entirely remove the effect of the filter from the face. If you don't, the face will seem distorted.

In this image below, titled *Artistic Bride*, the Dry Brush filter was applied to produce a painterly look. The image's color saturation was also increased using the Hue/Saturation command, the Burn tool, and the Saturation tool. Using the Clone tool, additional hair was added to the subject and the sculpture was removed from the table.

Original image (above) and final image (right)..

Heaven's Gate

After using the Dry Brush filter and printing the image on Epson's Watercolor Paper, it is impossible to tell that this image, called *Heaven's Gate*, was not originally painted with watercolors. As you'll see, some compositing was also used to create the final look of the image.

Original images (Heaven's Gate).

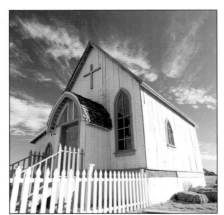

1. I began by opening the image of the church in Photoshop.
2. Then, I added the flowers to the photo, sizing them to fit by the fence hitting Ctrl/Cmd + T to open the Free Transform tool.
3. Once the two images were combined, the layers were flattened.

Heaven's Gate

4. Next, I hit Ctrl/Cmd + J to make a copy of the background layer.

5. I went to Filter>Artistic>Dry Brush and adjusted the options until I liked the effect produced.

6. Because the filter was applied on its own layer, I could adjust the opacity of the layer to reduce the effect.

7. The image was then flattened, and an artistic frame was added using Extensis Photo Frames.

● FILTER TECHNIQUES: CROSSHATCH FILTER

Another filter that I use a lot is called the Crosshatch filter (Filter>Brush Strokes>Crosshatch). This filter is especially beautiful when printed on Epson watercolor or archival matte paper. It softens the image and adds an affect similar to the texture of paper.

In this image of a high school senior (facing page), I wanted to bring the focus to her eyes. Photographing from a position higher than the subject and shooting down at a angle while tilting the camera gave the image a unique look.

1. I began by opening the senior portrait in Photoshop.
2. Next, I converted the image to black & white using the Lab-color conversion instructions on pages 77–78.
3. I went to Filter>Brush Strokes>Crosshatch to apply the filter. (With this filter, you may have to zoom in on the image to see the effect.)
4. I then added a layer mask by clicking on the Add a Mask icon at the bottom of the Layers palette.
5. With black as the foreground color, I used the Brush tool to mask out and soften the effect of the filter around the eyes.
6. I finished the photo by applying an edge effect using Extensis Photo Frames.

Final image (Crosshatch Filter).

● FILTER TECHNIQUES: PHOTO FILTERS

In Photoshop CS, a new tool called Photo Filters was introduced (Image>Adjustments>Photo Filters). These are similar to traditional photography filters that are placed in front of the lens. With these Photoshop filters, you can now apply a warming or cooling filter *after* the shoot (right).

● FILTER TECHNIQUES: PLASTIC WRAP FILTER

The image below was used for the cover of *Focus on Imaging*, the magazine for photo lab, digital lab, and on-site imaging professionals. The original image was captured on film and an artistic filter called Plastic Wrap (Filter>Artistic>Plastic Wrap) was applied to the image to make the tomatoes glisten. It was then faded (Edit>Fade Filter) to produce a more subtle effect.

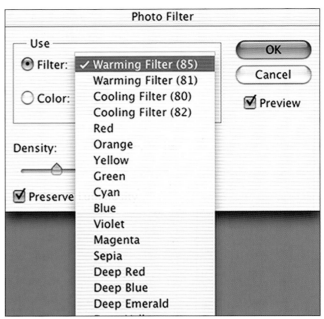

Photo filters (above) and final image with Plastic Wrap filter (below).

● FILTER TECHNIQUES: FRESCO FILTER

The image below, titled *Country Girl*, was captured digitally. It was artistically altered in Photoshop using the Fresco filter (Filter>Artistic>Fresco). The options for the filter were set to brush size: 1, brush detail: 6, and texture: 2. A layer mask was then added and the fresco effect was removed from the subject. Using the Fresco filter on the image added detail, texture, and contrast to the old wood, giving character to the image.

Original image (above) and final image (right) using the Fresco filter..

● FILTER TECHNIQUES: DIFFUSE GLOW FILTER

One of the filters I especially love for giving a beautiful glow to the image—almost the way infrared film looks—is the Diffuse Glow filter. In the portrait on the next page, the contemporary pose and style of the dress lent itself to a romantic yet edgy look. The image was captured with the Fuji S2 digital camera and manipulated in Photoshop.

The final bridal image with the Diffuse Glow effect applied.

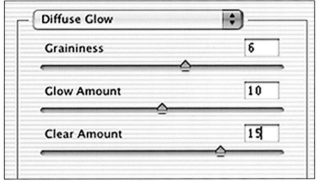

Figure 55.

1. To create this image, I began by opening the retouched image and making a copy of the background layer.
2. Next, I went to Filters>Brush Strokes>Crosshatch.
3. I clicked on the Add a Mask icon at the bottom of the Layers palette.
4. With the Brush tool set at 100-percent opacity, I used black to mask out the effect of the filter from the subject's eyes, nose and mouth.
5. Next, I merged the layer down (Layer>Merge Down) to the background.
6. I then made another copy of the background.
7. The next step was to add the Diffuse Glow filter (Filter>Distort>Diffuse Glow). The options for filter were set to graininess: 6, glow amount: 10, and clear amount: 15 (figure 55).
8. I lowered the opacity of the layer to 60 percent to make the effect more subtle.
9. I then merged down again, and then made another copy of the background layer. On the duplicated layer, I reapplied the Diffuse Glow filter and reduced the layer opacity, this time, to 39 percent.
10. The final step was to create the digital mat. I began by creating a new document the size of the finished print and filling it (Edit>Fill) with a color sampled from the image with the Eyedropper tool. Holding down the Shift key, I used the Move tool to transfer the image to the new document. I added a black stroke around the image by clicking on the Add a Layer Style icon at the bottom of the Layers palette. For the black stroke on the mat, I made a selection with the Rectangular Marquee tool, then went to Edit>Stroke and chose a black inside stroke at 8 pixels.
11. Finally, I flattened the final image for output.

In the image shown on the next page, the same Diffuse Glow filter gave the image a soft quality similar to infrared film, but without all the trouble it takes to capture an image using the traditional infrared technique. Here's the basic technique.

1. Open the image in Photoshop and make a copy of the background layer.
2. Change the blending mode of the layer to Soft Light.
3. Go to Filter>Distort>Diffuse Glow and apply the filter.

4. In the Styles palette, click on Blue Duotone to change the color of the print.

5. To finish the print, add a mat and stroke as described in step 10 of the previous technique.

In the previous two images, the Diffuse Glow works very well, but it also added a graininess to the photo that isn't always suitable when used for portraits. For a better way to add a "dream glow" to the skin, look at the examples presented in chapter 16 on retouching for glamour.

Original image (top) and final image (above) with the Diffuse Glow filter.

13. THE STYLES PALETTE

$\mathcal{U}$sing Photoshop's Styles palette, it has now become easier than ever before to add cool effects to your portraits. If the Styles palette is not visible on your screen, go to Window>Styles to bring it up. You may wish to click on the option arrow at the top right of the palette and choose Text Only. This will provide you with a text-only list of the styles available to you (you can choose to see thumbnails for each style, if you prefer). To append additional styles, go to the same menu and select Load Styles. A dialog box will appear, listing sets of styles you can load. After you have loaded the styles, you can then apply everything from a drop shadow, to a background texture, to a cool color filter with one click of the mouse.

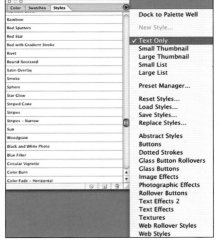

Viewing the styles in Text Only format can be useful.

● STYLES TECHNIQUES: COLLAGE

1. Set the background color to black, then create a new 8 x 8-inch document (File>New) to be used for the background. At the bottom of the dialog box, set the Background Contents to Background Color.

2. Open the original retouched image of the subject you plan to use.

3. Crop each image to 4 x 4-inches at the same resolution as the background you created in step 1.

4. With the Move tool, bring over the image into the black document.

5. Make three additional copies of the image layer by dragging them down to the Make a Copy icon at the bottom of your Layers palette.

6. Add a grid by going to View>Show>Grid. Align your images to the grid, with each image taking up a quarter of the total image area. You may wish to maximize your view of the image and zoom in to make sure the portraits line up correctly and are positioned side-by-side.

7. To change the look of each layer, go to the Styles palette (Window>Styles). Click on the style you prefer for the image layer you

have activated. Then, activate the next layer and continue to apply different styles.

8. Flatten the image (Layer>Flatten Image) and make a copy of the background layer.

9. In your Styles palette, select the style called Batik to add the look that you see on the background of the images in this example. Lower the opacity of the layer until you get the desired effect.

10. Use a layer mask to remove the Batik effect from the subject. The final effect will be like the one shown to the right.

Final image.

● STYLES TECHNIQUES: FRAMING TECHNIQUES

For the next example, I used the Screened Luminosity style as a framing effect for the image and the Color Burn style to add depth to the photo.

1. In Photoshop, open a retouched image (figure 56).
2. Make a copy of the background and select the Color Burn style from the Styles palette. This will darken the image.
3. Add a layer mask. Using the Brush tool set at 100-percent opacity (with black set as the foreground color) paint over the face to mask

Figures 56 (left) and 57 (right).

Final image for Framing Techniques (top left). The same simple technique was used in the bridal portrait shown at the bottom left of the page. The only step not used was the addition of the Color Burn style.

out the Color Burn effect that was applied to the subject and shirt. (Remember: black takes away; white adds back.)

4. Merge down the later to the background (Layer>Merge Down).

5. Go to View>Show>Grid.

6. Make a uniform selection around the image using the Rectangular Marquee tool.

7. Hit Ctrl/Cmd + I to inverse the selection.

8. Then, hit Ctrl/Cmd + J to move the selected area to its own layer.

9. In the Styles palette, select the Screen Luminosity style. Then merge down the later to the background (Layer>Merge) (figure 57).

10. For the final presentation, a stroke was added around the image and the image was put on a green mat (top left).

● **STYLES TECHNIQUES: DIGITAL ALBUM DESIGN**

The following image, titled *Makeover Madness,* was created for a client's digital wedding album. It is a great example of how easy it is to design a digital album using the Styles palette. These albums offer

the client a more artistic design with a variety of text, artistic effects, and colors. I used the following steps to create the collage of the bride getting ready.

Final image (Digital Album Design; Make-over Madness).

1. In Photoshop, create a new document by going to File>New. This document will be used as the background of the image, so set the size and resolution as needed for your final output.

2. Open the color-corrected images you plan to use for the collage. Making sure they are at the same resolution as the background.

3. For a 10 x 10-inch collage for an album page that includes nine images, crop each image to 3 x 3 inches.

4. With the Move tool, bring each image over, one by one, into the background file.

5. Check the Auto Select Layer box in the Options bar of the Move tool to selectively move each image into the desired location with the Move tool.

6. After you have moved all the images to your background, add a grid by going to View>Show>Grid. Zoom in on the image to make sure your images line up correctly.

7. To easily change the look of each layer, go to the Styles palette. Click on the style you prefer for the image you have activated. Activate the next image by clicking on it, then add another style. Continue adding styles until you have completed each image.

8. At this point, you can also change the color of your background. To do this, select a color in the Color palette and use the Paint Bucket tool fill your background.

9. Save your collage as a PSD file (without flattening the layers) so that you can make any future changes that are needed.

● STYLES TECHNIQUES: RAIN EFFECT

This image was created in the studio but changed in Photoshop to look like the subject is standing out in the rain on a very stormy day. The rain is very easily applied in the Styles palette.

1. Open a color image of a child taken in the studio on a plain, dark background.
2. Hit Ctrl/Cmd + J to make a copy of the layer.
3. In the Styles palette, click on the style called Black & White Photo.
4. Add a mask to this layer by clicking on the Add a Mask icon at the bottom of the Layers palette.
5. With black as the foreground color, use the Brush tool at 100-percent opacity to mask out the black & white style, bringing back the color of the subject.
6. Merge the two layers together by going to the side arrow (at the upper-right corner) of the Layers palette and choosing Merge Down.
7. Press Ctrl/Cmd + J to make a copy of the image on a new layer.
8. Return to the Styles palette and click on the style called Rain.
9. Reduce the effect of the rain, if needed, by lowering the opacity of the layer.
10. Flatten the image.
11. In this example, an artistic edge from Extensis Photo Frames was added to complete the image.

Final image (Rain Effect).

● STYLES TECHNIQUES: HOT BURST COLLAGE

I used the Styles palette for the image, titled *Pixel and Bond*, which was used as a marketing piece for a contest that we put on our web site (www.ferrophotographyschool.com). As you can see, the image was a lot of fun to photograph and the addition of the Hot Burst effect gave the impression that it could have been a movie poster.

Phase One

1. In Photoshop, go to File>New and select a size for the new document, which will be the background of the entire image. Set the Background Contents to white.
2. In the Color palette, select a deep royal blue for the foreground color.
3. Go to Edit>Fill to fill the white document with the foreground color.
4. Hit Ctrl/Cmd + J to make a copy of the layer.
5. In the Styles palette, choose Hot Burst to create a vivid spray of color.

Phase Two

1. Extract the image of the subjects by going to Filter>Extract.
2. With the Highlighter tool in the Extract dialog box, carefully trace around the outline of the subjects with green set in the Highlight field (figure 58).
3. Click on the subjects with the Fill tool in the Extract dialog box.
4. Click OK to extract.
5. With the Move tool, drag the extracted image over to the Hot Burst background.
6. Add text as desired.

Original image (Hot Burst Collage).

Figure 58.

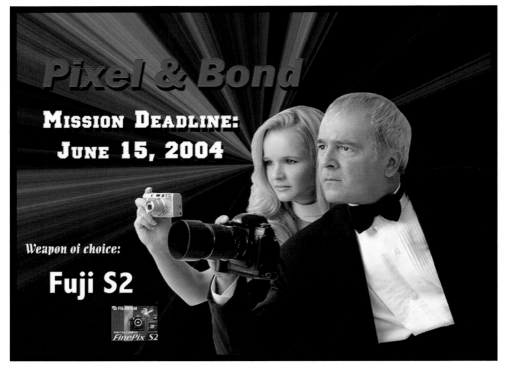

Final image.

Drawing requires an understanding of shape, form, and anatomy.

*T*he development of drawing as a form of artistic expression, rather than a mere recording of compositional ideas, has evolved from caves, to frescos, to wax tablets, to paper, to the computer. With advanced software technology, drawing can be achieved through non-traditional methods. Virtual sketching provides the artist with limitless possibilities.

I started drawing artistically before the age of eight. My parents noticed my interest and gave me an art kit for Christmas that I will never forget. That little kit started me on a track of art lessons and creative vision. Art was always my favorite subject in school. Drawing has always been the foundation for anything that I have done artistically. Painting, especially when it involves portraits, usually involves drawing a basic sketch in which to lay the foundation. You will also notice in traditional painting, especially watercolor, that the sketch remains underneath the color, showing through the paint.

Whether drawing from memory, a photograph, or the subject in front of you, drawing requires an understanding of shape, form, and anatomy. It also takes lots of practice. For the serious sketch artist, Photoshop's Illustrator is the software of choice. However, both Photoshop and Painter also support drawing.

● **DRAWING TECHNIQUES: A BASIC SKETCH**

In Painter, you can make a clone of the photograph and turn on the tracing paper to help you create a sketch. The image used to demonstrate this technique is called *The Butterfly*.

1. In Painter, open your image and go to File>Clone to make an exact duplicate (a clone copy) of the original.

2. Select the image by choosing Select>All. Then hit Delete. At this point, the photograph will turn into a white canvas.

3. Next, press Ctrl/Cmd + T to toggle on the tracing paper. (You can also click on the top-right corner of the document window to turn on the tracing paper.)

4. At this point, with the tracing paper turned on, you can

begin to sketch from the original photograph. By choosing the Pen tool and one of the Scratchboard variants, you can begin creating a sketch.

5. You can also add additional layers and drag them so that they underlay the sketch. This allows you to paint on individual layers without affecting the sketch.

6. In this case, color was added to each layer to create the final image.

7. For the final image, I kept the sketch layer intact, because I liked the outlining effect it provided. However, I could have eliminated the sketch and merely used it as a guide for painting.

In Painter, you can also turn photos into sketches by going to Effects> Surface Control>Sketch. This converts the image to a quick basic sketch.

Original image for A Basic Sketch (top left), image in progress (top right), and final image (above).

● DRAWING TECHNIQUES: COLORIZED LINE DRAWING

This Photoshop technique is great to use for high-school senior images.

1. In Photoshop, open an image (facing page, top).

2. Go to Image>Mode>Grayscale to discard the color information.

3. Drag your background layer to the Create a New Layer icon at the bottom of the Layers palette to make a copy of it.

4. Invert layer by going Image>Adjustments>Invert. Then, change the mode of the overlying layer to Color Dodge. The image will seem to fade completely.

5. Go to Filter>Blur>Gaussian Blur and set the radius to about 10 pixels (this is what brings back detail, so the exact setting to use will depend on the image). Flatten the image.

Original image (Colorized Line Drawing).

Figure 59 (left) and final image (below).

6. Go to Image>Mode>RGB.

7. Make a copy of the background layer and change the blending mode to Multiply to darken the lines. Flatten the image.

8. Make a copy of the background layer for your first paint layer.

9. Choose the Brush tool and set its blending mode to Color. Selecting a color from the Color Picker, paint on the image. Don't worry about going outside the lines.

10. Add a layer mask. Using black, mask out any areas where you went outside the lines.

11. Flatten the image and repeat steps 8 and 9 as needed (figure 59).

12. Choose the Brush tool and set its blending mode to Normal and its opacity to 100 percent. Select a color from the Color Picker and paint on a new layer. Add a new layer for each area you paint, so that you can adjust the layer opacities to reduce the intensity of the colors.

13. Add a layer mask. Using black, mask out any areas where you went outside the lines.

14. Repeat steps 12 and 13 until all areas are colored.

15. Before flattening the image, multiply the layers as needed to achieve the desired effect. Flatten the image.

● DRAWING TECHNIQUES: PENCIL SKETCHES FROM PHOTOGRAPHS

1. In Photoshop, open a flattened image (figure 60).

2. Go to Image>Mode>Grayscale (figure 61).

3. Make a copy of the background layer by dragging it onto the Create a New Layer icon at the bottom of the Layers palette.

4. Hit Ctrl/Cmd + I to invert the image (figure 62), then change the blend mode of the overlying layer to Color Dodge (at the top of the Layers palette). The image will look like it has disappeared, but the next step will bring it back.

5. Go to Filter>Blur>Gaussian Blur. Adjust the radius until you see enough detail in the image to represent a pencil sketch (figure 63).

6. Flatten the image, and then make a copy of the background by dragging it onto the Add a Layer icon at the bottom of the Layers palette.

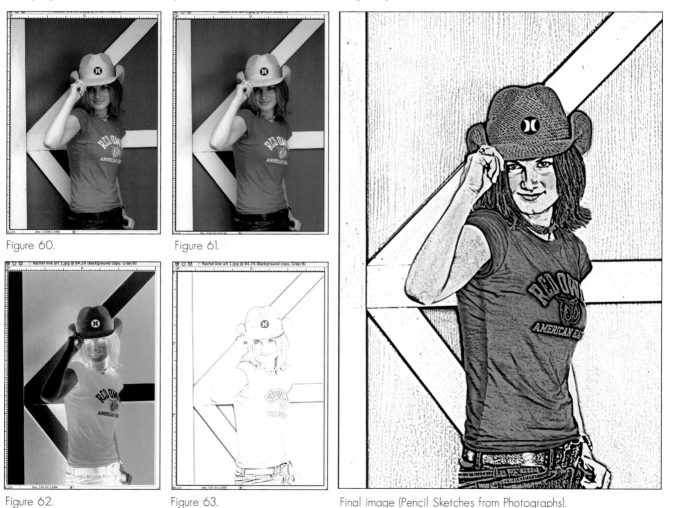

Figure 60.

Figure 61.

Figure 62.

Figure 63.

Final image (Pencil Sketches from Photographs).

7. Change the blend mode of the top layer to Multiply. This will darken the "sketch" lines.

8. Flatten the image.

9. Go to Image>Mode>RGB. (You cannot color an image while it is in the Grayscale mode.)

10. Click on the Create a New Layer icon at the bottom of the Layers palette. Set the blend mode of this layer to Color.

11. Select the colors that you want to paint the image with. Then, with the Brush tool, color your image as you desire, altering the opacity of your Brush tool as you like.

Final image (Colored Pencil Drawing).

● **DRAWING TECHNIQUES: COLORED PENCIL DRAWING**

1. In Photoshop, open an image.

2. Go to Filter>Stylize>Find Edges.

3. Drag the background layer onto the Create a New Layer icon at the bottom of the Layers palette to create a copy.

4. Change the blend mode of the new layer to Multiply.

5. To darken the image more, continue to make copies of your layer by hitting Ctrl/Cmd + J. (The new layers should also be in the Multiply blend mode.)

6. Flatten the image.

15. COOL EFFECTS

Digital imaging has made it easy to create some cool effects. We'll explore some creative effects in this chapter, but don't hesitate to try out your own variations and ideas. You should always be on the lookout for techniques that can enhance your images.

● COOL TECHNIQUES: FUNKY CHIC

As with many of my images, when I started creating this portrait, titled *Funky Chic,* I didn't exactly know where I was going with the image until I start working on it. In cases like this, I start by visualizing the possibilities and experimenting with different approaches until I end up with a finished design that I am pleased with. The steps I used when creating this image are as follows.

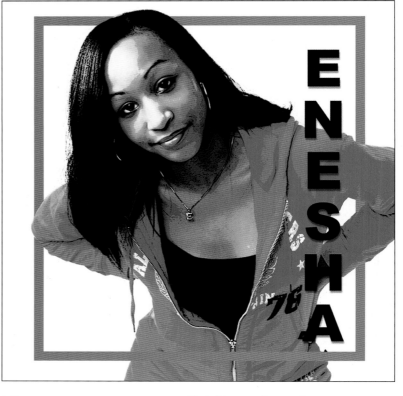

Digital imaging has made it easy to create some cool effects.

1. Working in Photoshop, I began with a color-corrected image of the subject and duplicated the background layer.
2. Next, I applied glamour retouching to the face (see chapter 16).
3. To create a more appealing outline that better fit the subject, the coat on the subject's shoulder and arm was adjusted with the Liquify filter (Filter>Liquify) (figure 64).
4. Using an adjustment layer, I opened up the Curves window and raised individual points on the curve until the colors of the coat and hat were changed from the original black and brown tones.

5. Next, I removed this effect from the face, body, and background using a layer mask and painting on it with the Brush tool set at 100-percent opacity and the foreground color set to black (figure 65).

6. I merged this adjustment layer down to the retouched layer.

7. Then, I made a new copy of the retouched layer.

8. To create the design on the background, I added the Batik effect from the Style palette. After clicking on the style, I lowered the opacity of the layer until I achieved the look I wanted.

9. Next, I added a layer mask to the image by clicking on the Add a Mask icon at the bottom of the Layers palette.

Original image (Funky Chic).

Figure 64.

Figure 65.

10. With the Brush tool set to black with 100-percent opacity, I removed the Batik style from the subject, so that it remained only on the background (bottom image, previous page).

● COOL TECHNIQUES: INCREASED HIGHLIGHTS

This senior's original image showed acne and blemishes. By changing the image's highlights using the Curves in Photoshop, the blemishes were removed (right).

Final image (Increased Highlights).

1. Open your image.
2. Click on the Add Adjustment Layer icon at the bottom of the Layers palette and choose Curves.
3. When the Curves dialog box comes up, drag the midpoint of the curve up to blow out the highlights and watch all the blemishes disappear.
4. On the adjustment layer's built-in layer mask, use your Brush tool (with black set at the foreground color) to mask out any of the Curves adjustment that you do not wish to retain.

In both of the images below, the highlights were purposely blown out to create a fashion look that softens the skin and renders a trendy effect. The image on the left was overexposed in the camera, as previously dis-

Overexposed in the camera.

Overexposed in Photoshop.

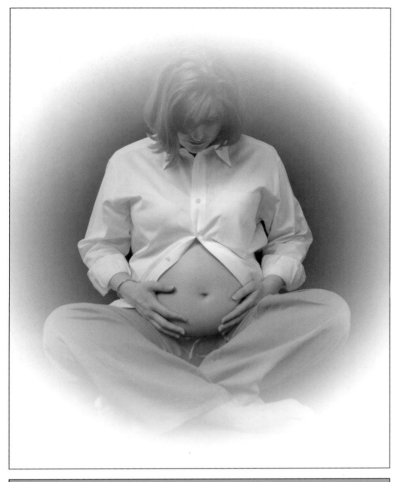

In this beautiful image of an expectant mother (left), a low opacity effect was created using the Circular Vignette from Photoshop's Styles palette.

Final image for Low-Opacity Background (bottom left).

cussed in chapter 10. The image on the right was overexposed using the technique in Photoshop for increasing the highlights (as noted above).

● COOL TECHNIQUES:
LOW-OPACITY BACKGROUND

1. In Photoshop, create a new file with a white background by going to File>New.
2. Enter the desired size and resolution for the final image.
3. Open the image that you plan to use for the background.
4. Activate the Move tool and, holding down your Shift key to center it precisely, drag it over into your new document.
5. In the Styles palette, click on Screened Luminosity to create a low-opacity background.
6. Go back to your original image and resize or crop it as needed to serve at the main image that will appear over the low-opacity background.
7. With your Move tool activated, drag this image over into the document with your background image.
8. At this point, you can refine the size of the overlying image by hitting Ctrl/Cmd + T. Hold down the Shift key as you drag the slider to avoid distortion.
9. To add a stroke and/or a drop shadow, hit the Add a Layer Style button at the bottom of the Layers palette and choose the desired effect (final image, left).

Using a large amount of Unsharp Masking actually finds the edges and can improve definition where it was lacking.

● COOL TECHNIQUES: OVERSHARPENING

While this technique is not appropriate for portraits, for fine art and land-scapes, I sometimes use the Unsharp Mask filter at an increased setting (amount: 500 percent, radius: 50 pixels, threshold: 50). This large amount of Unsharp Masking actually finds the edges and can improve definition where it was lacking—especially in an overexposed image. As a result, the image looks almost as though it was colored with colored pencils, or pen and ink. The same technique can also be paired with an increase in the hue and saturation of the image to give the look of gouache paint.

1. Open an image in Photoshop.
2. Hit Ctrl/Cmd + J to make a copy of the image.
3. Go to Filter>Sharpen>Unsharp Mask.
4. In the Unsharp Mask dialog box, change the settings to amount: 500, threshold: 50, and radius: 50.
5. The effect can be decreased, if you wish, by lowering the opacity of the layer.
6. Flatten the layers (Layer>Flatten Image).

16. RETOUCHING FOR GLAMOUR

Glamour retouching involves digitally applying makeup to the photograph to change the look of the subject in order to achieve the "glamour" look.

*C*lients today are influenced by the fashion and glamour photography that they see in television, movies, and fashion magazines. Therefore, glamour retouching is different than the basic retouching that may be needed for the average portrait client. In addition to removing flaws, it involves digitally applying makeup to the photograph to change the look of the subject in order to achieve the "glamour" look.

Having the basic knowledge of the structure of the face is important when applying makeup (whether you are using cosmetics or, in this case, pixels). Understanding the curves, indentations, and planes of the face will allow you to creatively alter the photograph to produce a whole new look.

The application of makeup can enhance or detract from the face's natural shape, creating startling and dramatic results. My retouching approach, however, is to make the subject look fresher and feel better about their appearance, *without* dramatically altering the individual's true characteristics.

When photographing with a glamour portrait in mind, I always ask the subject to arrive at the studio with their foundation and basic makeup applied. It is much easier to add makeup digitally than it is to take it away, so this simple application of makeup gives you a clean canvas to start applying your glamour makeup digitally.

● BASIC TECHNIQUES

When retouching, I always work on a copy of the background layer. As I work, I make additional copies, apply the desired technique, then merge down. By keeping two layers instead of multiple ones, I can work quickly—and I can always use a layer mask to restore the original image if needed. I can also reduce the layer opacity to make the effect more subtle.

● HEALING BRUSH AND CLONE STAMP

The Healing and Patch tools are by far my favorites, but I also use the Clone tool, Burn and Dodge tools, and the Brush tool. There are several ways to retouch a portrait. The following are just a few of the choices that I prefer:

Healing Brush

To eliminate imperfections you can use Photoshop's Healing Brush.

1. Working on a copy of your background layer, activate the Healing Brush tool in the Toolbar.
2. Press Alt/Opt and left click to sample an area of similar color as the area to be concealed.
3. Release the Alt/Opt key and move your cursor over the blemish, then left click to remove the blemish. (If you are using a graphics tablet, you will merely touch the blemish with your stylus after determining your sample point.)
4. Because the Healing Brush tool samples and blends from surrounding pixels, if you are close to an area of different color, it will bring those in as well. Therefore, it isn't the answer in every situation.

The original image (top) was retouched (middle) then cropped and converted to black & white for the final presentation (above).

Clone Stamp Tool

1. After eliminating the majority of blemishes with the Healing Brush tool, I like to go over the face (especially a woman's face) with the Clone Stamp tool set to 20- to 22-percent opacity.
2. After activating the Clone tool in the Toolbar, change the opacity (in the options bar at the top of your screen) to 22 percent.
3. Select a nearby area of the skin that is lighter than the area you want to retouch, then press Alt/Opt and left click to sample the lighter

area. With a medium brush size, sweep over the darker area to lighten it and smooth it out.

4. Continue this method around the face, sampling areas as needed.

Adding Makeup To The Eyes and Lips

1. To add makeup to the eyes and lips, I select the Burn tool.

2. With the smallest brush possible and an exposure setting of 10 percent, I outline the lashes and the line of the eyes and lips.

3. Depending on the image, you may need to increase the Burn tool's exposure setting to make it darker and achieve the look you want.

Adding Color To The Face

When adding color to the cheeks, or to give the entire face a glow, use the Brush tool as follows:

1. Activate the Brush tool and, in the options bar at the top of the screen, click the Enable Airbrush Capabilities icon.

2. Then, set the tool to the color mode (also in the options bar).

3. Finally, set its opacity to 2- to 10-percent.

4. Double click on the foreground color at the bottom of the Toolbar. When the Color Picker box appears, select a soft red and click OK.

5. With a large, soft brush, sweep over the areas of the face to which you want to add either cheek color or a warm glow.

Original image (India Eyes).

● RETOUCHING TECHNIQUES: INDIA EYES

Glamour Retouching

1. I began by opening the original image in Photoshop (top left).

2. Then, I made a copy of the background layer.

3. Using the Healing Brush tool, I cleaned up the blemishes (figure 66).

4. Dragging this layer to the Create a New Layer icon at the bottom of the Layers palette, I created a copy of the image.

Figure 66.

5. I used the Patch tool under the eyes, then reduced the opacity of the overlying layer in the Layers palette to keep the shape and color under the eyes, which is consistent with Indian skin tones (figure 67).

6. I merged down this layer.

7. Next, I created a copy of the previous layer by dragging it onto the Create a New Layer icon at the bottom of the Layers palette.

8. Using the Clone tool set at 20-percent opacity, I cleaned up the eyebrows.

Figure 67.

9. Using the Dodge tool, I created a half-moon shape in the iris of the eye and dodged the whites of the eye to take away some, but not all, of the red. Using the Burn tool at a low opacity, I increased the detail in eyelashes and circled the ring of the iris of the eye (figure 68).

10. Then, with the Clone Stamp tool set at medium to low opacity, I cleaned up the areas on her lip that looked like she had been biting it. When retouching lips, be careful that you do not take out all of the little creases and texture in the mouth (figure 69.

11. To give it a painterly look, I used the Clone Stamp tool over entire face at 20-percent opacity, making sure the sample point was as close as possible to the area that I was covering, so that I didn't move dark areas into light and light areas into dark. This process smoothed out the skin without losing texture. It gave a more painterly appearance than the application of a Gaussian blur (figure 70).

12. I merged down this layer.

Figure 68.

Figure 69.

Figure 70.

Additional Image Editing

At this point, the retouching of the face is complete. However, some additional refinements need to be made to create the strongest possible presentation. Although these don't necessarily fall into category of glamour retouching, for teaching purposes, I would like to discuss the techniques used to accomplish them.

First, I used the Patch tool to clean up any areas of the background that were distracting or had light spill on them.

Next, I turned my attention to her hand. If there were other images of her in the dress without the hand showing, it would have been ideal to bring over the portion of the image that would match the veil and merge the two images to remove the hand. Lacking such an image, however, doesn't make the task impossible. To correct the problem, I used the Lasso tool to select a small piece of the edge of the hand. Then, I clicked inside the selection and moved it over a nearby area of the blue fabric. I copied this material to a new layer, then moved it over the hand where I took the sample and used the Levels (Image>Adjustments>Levels) to adjust its tonality to blend with the fabric around it and merged it down to the previous later. I repeated this process until I had completely covered the hand. Then, I used the Patch and Healing Brush tools to blend the pieces of fabric together and make the area appear more realistic.

To add a medallion, the print in the fabric, I selected the medallion at the bottom of the image using the Lasso tool and put it on its own layer by hitting Ctrl/Cmd + J. Using the Free Transform tool (Ctrl/Cmd + T), I moved it and transformed it until it looked realistic.

Finally, I was ready to polish off the image, making the tones more dramatic. To do this, I created a Levels adjustment layer to darken the image. On the adjustment layer's layer mask, I painted with black to restore selected areas of the original image. This allowed me to paint shadows onto the subject's face and the background.

Final image.

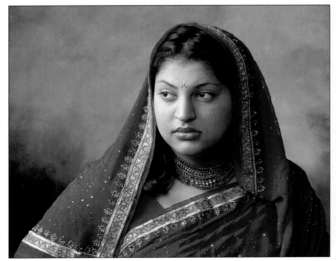 

This presentation was so successful that another client actually saw the image at a gallery showing, and commissioned me to create a photographic fine-art portrait of her in the same fashion! Original image (left) and final image (right).

● RETOUCHING TECHNIQUES: DREAM GLOW

In this example, the subject's skin was softened through a combination of blending modes and blurring. It is a technique I adapted from Scott Kelby's book *The Photoshop CS Book for Digital Photographers* (New Riders Press, 2003).

1. Open a retouched image that you want to soften.

2. Hit Ctrl/Cmd + J two times to make two exact copies of your original image. In the Layers palette, click on the Layer Visibility icon (the eyeball) for the top layer copy to make it invisible. Then, click on the middle layer to make it active.

3. In the Layers palette, switch the blend mode to Darken.

4. While still on the middle layer, go to Filter>Blur>Gaussian Blur and apply a 40-pixel blur to the image (figure 71).

5. In the Layers palette, make the middle layer invisible. Activate the top layer by clicking on it, then change the blend mode to Lighten.

Original image.

Figure 71

Figure 72

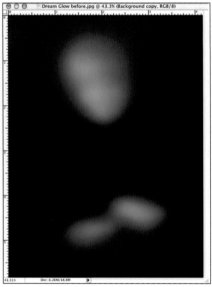

Figure 73

6. While still on the top layer, go to Filter>Blur>Gaussian Blur and add a 60-pixel blur to the layer (figure 72).

7. Go back to the middle later and lower its opacity to 40 percent. (Don't give up! It really *is* worth all of these steps!)

8. Make the background layer invisible by clicking off the Layer Visibility icon. Add a new blank layer by clicking on the Create a New Layer icon at the bottom of the Layers palette. Drag this layer to the top of your Layers palette. Holding down the Alt/Opt key, go to Layer>Merge Visible (figure 73).

Final image.

9. Click back on the eyeball of the background layer to make it visible again and hide the two middle layers by clicking off the eyeball next to them.

10. Activate the top layer by clicking on it and lower the opacity of the layer to 40 percent. This creates a beautiful effect on the face, softening the skin.

11. At this point, you'll want to sharpen the eyes and mouth by using a layer mask to mask out the glow over these areas, returning them to sharpness.

If you regularly use a technique like this in your production workflow, you should create an action to eliminate the lengthy steps it take to achieve the end result.

● RETOUCHING TECHNIQUES: TWO HEADS ARE BETTER THAN ONE

In the images below, glamour lighting was achieved by using a 3 x 5-foot Larson softbox placed directly over Lori and set at f/16. On both images, a hair light (set a f/5.6) and a kicker light (set at f/4.0) were used. In the first image (left), a black felt background was used from SkyHigh Backgrounds without a background light and the camera was set at f/16 to match the soft box. In the second image (right), a white background was used with additional lights to render the background gray. The camera was set at f/13 so that the image would be overexposed, producing a soft, dewy skin tone. In both images, a eye-lighter from Larry Peters was used to achieve a half-moon highlight in the eye.

Two original images were used to create the final presentation (Two Heads Are Better Than One).

Once the image was captured, it was brought into Photoshop and the face from the second image was selected with the Lasso tool and put on its own layer by hitting Ctrl/Cmd + J. It was then transferred to the first image and positioned. The Healing Brush tool was used to smooth out the transition between the face and Lori's hairline. Using a Wacom Tablet and a graphics pen, Lori's makeup was then enhanced using a variety of retouching methods, including burning and dodging the eyes, shaping the lips with the Brush tool, and smoothing out the skin with the Clone Stamp tool set at 20-percent opacity. Lori's face was then reduced in size using the Liquify filter to achieve a more flattering appearance. The last step was to darken the background using a Levels adjustment layer.

Since Lori needed a business card, we made the decision that turning her portrait into a black & white image would yield greater impact for professional use. The conversion was done using the Lab color conversion method discussed in chapter 11. As you can see, the result is a beautiful image and a professional business card that Lori can be proud of!

Final image.

17. SELLING AND MARKETING YOUR FINE-ART PIECE

*Y*ou can have an incredible talent for digital artistry and produce beautiful works of art, but the challenge of marketing and selling your work can still be a big one. Unless you have been commissioned to do a special piece for your client, the marketing of digital art takes a different slant than the marketing for the average portrait studio. It takes more than being a talented photographic artist to become a successful professional artist in the business of fine art. Beyond creating the *art*, you have to understand the *business*.

● MARKETING

The challenge with our profession is to successfully merge the passion for art with a smart business plan. Most photographic artists would prefer to spend all their time expressing their creative vision rather than doing the accounting tasks or marketing chores that turn art into profit. To be financially successful, it takes both. Success doesn't just happen; you have to make it happen.

Show Your Work. The best way to make the community aware of your artwork is to show it. As we know in the portrait business, you sell what you show! Most people think of art galleries as the first place to try to display their work, but that's not necessarily true. Other places that the public traffics on a regular basis—restaurants, hair salons, malls, etc.—are great for showcasing your fine art and are often overlooked as an opportunity for exposure. Consider other opportunities, as well—like universities, libraries, banks, and office lobbies.

Market to Other Professionals. Another great way of marketing your work is to barter with other professionals that have need of your service. For example, visit the places that you do regular business with (hair salons, restaurants, etc.) and see if they will allow you to provide your services in

> The challenge is to successfully merge the passion for art with a smart business plan.

Lou Gardens

Do your research and find out which gallery offers the best representation of your style.

exchange for them displaying your work. You can offer to give them a complimentary portrait session, for instance. Interior designers and architects may have need of your work for display to highlight their services. By marketing your work through cards or displayed artwork at their business location, you can increase your client base.

Why not have a wine and cheese opening at a frame shop? You can display your art pieces and meet the locals that will, hopefully, be your future customers! Partner with a frame shop that will advertise your work, displaying it in some of their frames. Share the costs on the advertising, since it benefits both of you.

Galleries. There are also commercial galleries, which charge a commission on sales, and artist co-op galleries, which usually require membership to exhibit your work. Do your research and find out which venue offers the best representation of your style. Also, inquire as to interview opportunities and what their display requirements are.

The Worldwide Web. The web is a great place for getting your images out to the community in your area—and to the world as well! If you are not able to dedicate a web site to your fine art, then join web sites that will not only show your work, but spend the time to put you before the right search engines. Either way, there is a cost involved. Two web sites to look at are www.artspan.com and www.globalart.net. Become active online and establish an e-mail presence. Make it a point to talk with other professionals involved in the business of art—gallery owners or managers, museum curators, art critics, professors of art, professional framers, etc. These people will have information and ideas for locations of exhibition space.

Media and Organizations. Press releases are an option, but often yield minimal results. However, writing an article for your community paper about art draws more interest. Make yourself available to the community. Join the Chamber of Commerce in your area. Auctions are a great

Partner with a frame shop that will advertise your work, displaying it in some of their frames.

A limited-edition print creates more perceived value to the client.

place to get started showing your work because of the kind of clientele that comes to these events. Speak to the local women's club about art and photography, and mention where your art is being displayed. Self-promotion is the best way to get your work noticed.

Limited Editions. You can sign your work and create a limited-edition print that creates more perceived value to the client. The best way to do this is to set a number of prints, say 100, and then number each print in the series to reflect this, which will increase the value of the print. Limited-edition prints are numbered individually and are printed in quantity; thus, the numbering "4/295" would indicate that the print is the fourth in an edition of 295.

● PRICING

When pricing your fine art, keep in mind that value is sometimes determined by price. Photographers are notorious for underpricing their work. Determining the cost of your art piece is a good starting point. The time it takes to create a custom art piece needs to be reflected in the price, as does the total number of prints that you will sell from this original piece. If your artwork has been marketed well, to be considered as fine art and not just digital photography, the consumer will perceive it to have more value.

Sometimes it is advantageous to do speculation work for clients when you see the possibilities from a particular session.

Display the Price. Make it easy for the client to buy. Displaying your work is not enough if there is no price on it. Too many times I have seen works of art displayed in restaurants and wanted to know the price. I was given the artist's business card, but when I got home I didn't take the time to call the artist and ask the price. So, make sure that you definitely have a price on your work.

Speculation Work. Sometimes it is even advantageous to do speculation work for clients when you see the possibilities from a particular session. The image to the left was done on speculation for the client. The preferred method of selling fine-art images to the studio client is to charge an artistic fee on top of your normal print prices. A portrait oil artist could easily charge thousands of dollars for their work, so why shouldn't we?

● DONATE YOUR CRAFT

We are in business to not just to take images but also to make money. Still, we should always remember how blessed we are to be able to make a living doing what we love. One of the ways my husband Rick and I try to return a small portion of what we have been blessed with is to donate our craft. The image below was taken of a child who was not expected to live. The image was displayed at the baby's funeral one week after presenting it to the family. The mother herself was still a child and the image, titled *Angel Babies,* has impacted everyone who has seen it. It was an honor and joy to be part of this family's gift of knowing this child—even for such a short time. Remember, always, that we are blessed with a talent that few hold. It is our responsibility to share it with the world.

One of the ways my husband Rick and I try to return a small portion of what we have been blessed with is to donate our craft.

page 15

page 25

page 45

page 10

page 51

page 23

page 24

page 21

page 17

page 36

page 77

page 31

page 49

page 16

page 37

page 30

page 41

page 26

page 55

page 47

page 52

page 41

page 67

page 68

page 90

INDEX

ABOUT THE AUTHOR

Deborah Lynn Ferro holds a masters degree in photography from Wedding and Portrait Photographers International (WPPI) and her Craftsman's degree from Professional Photographers of America (PPA). She has extensive training in Photoshop and is a member of National Association of Photoshop Professionals (NAPP). Deborah is currently teaching around the country, and her popular class called "Practical Photoshop Techniques for Photographers," draws large classes of professional photographers. With her husband Rick Ferro, also an acclaimed wedding and portrait photographer, Deborah is the coauthor of *Wedding Photography with Adobe Photoshop* (also from Amherst Media). For more on Deborah Lynn Ferro, visit www.ferrophotographyschool.com.

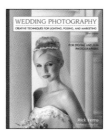
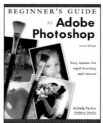
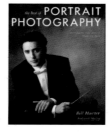
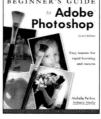